Whose Permission Are You Waiting For?

Whose Permission Are You Waiting For?

An Educator's Guide to Doing What You Love

William D. Parker

ConnectEDD Publishing
Hanover, Pennsylvania

Copyright © 2025 by William D. Parker

All rights reserved. No part of this publication may be reproduced, distributed, or transmitted in any form or by any means, including photocopying, recording, or other electronic or mechanical methods, without the prior written permission of the publisher, except in the case of brief quotations embodied in critical reviews and certain other noncommercial uses permitted by copyright law. For permission requests, contact the publisher at: info@connecteddpublishing.com

This publication is available at discount pricing when purchased in quantity for educational purposes, promotions, or fundraisers. For inquiries and details, contact the publisher at: info@connecteddpublishing.com

Published by ConnectEDD Publishing LLC
Hanover, PA
www.connecteddpublishing.com

Cover Design: Kheila Casas

Whose Permission Are You Waiting For? —1st ed. Paperback
ISBN 979-8-9918506-3-6

Praise for *Whose Permission Are You Waiting For?*

William D. Parker has done it again! This book is an empowering guide for educators looking to break the mold and discover fulfilling career paths beyond the traditional classroom. It provides practical advice, emphasizing self-reflection, exploration, and consistent action to achieve professional goals. A must-read for any educator seeking a change!

–Dr. Jen Schwanke | Author, Educator, Deputy Superintendent, Dublin City Schools, Dublin, Ohio

William D. Parker presents a masterful guide for educators seeking fulfillment and impact in their careers. With a rich history of leadership and a compassionate approach, Will deftly navigates the complexities of the educational landscape, offering both practical strategies and heartfelt wisdom. Each chapter is a testament to his deep commitment to fostering growth, not just in students but in educators themselves. From understanding pathways in education to the value of coaching and reflective practices, Parker's insights are both profound and actionable. William D. Parker's compassionate and strategic approach is bound to inspire and empower educators everywhere.

–John Marinucci | St Francis College, Crestmead, Queensland, Australia

What I appreciated most is that this book reads like a novel, blending lessons with Will's diverse experiences. Whether you're a new or veteran leader, each chapter offers a compelling story and practical strategies for continued growth. You can open any chapter that speaks to you and find encouragement to take initiative and lead with purpose. If you're looking for inspiration, reflection, and actionable guidance, take Will up on his invitation. It's a walk well worth taking.

–Brent Kline | Palo Alto High School, Palo Alto, California

Will and I both began our careers as high school English teachers—a role that allowed us the privilege of helping students acknowledge and seize the power of their stories. Practicing what he preaches, Will takes us on an episodic walk through his journey—a journey teeming with experiences, experiments, and epiphanies. I don't always remember facts, studies, or statistics, but I do remember stories. They make lessons stickier. Will narrates it all—loss and leadership, faith and fear—and ultimately convinces us we've got to take care of ourselves if we wish to take care of others. Read it for yourself and the people who mean the most.

–Lisa Parry, M.Ed. | Principal, Teacher, Education Consultant, Arlington School District 38, Arlington, South Dakota

This book encourages readers to take risks and align their actions with their core values to lead authentically. It's a powerful call to stop waiting and start creating the work and life you love!

–Dr. Rachel Edoho-Eket | Principal, Author, Speaker

There is no one better than Will Parker for inspiring school leaders! Through classic "Will" stories and backed by research, *Whose Permission Are You Waiting For?* guides the reader on how to grow as a leader and increase their sphere of influence. Each chapter ends with great reflections that have helped me pause and be more intentional about my work. This is the education book I've been waiting for someone to write!

–Nick Davies, Ph.D. | 2024 AWSP Elementary Assistant Principal of the Year

Will has managed to weave stories, research and practical advice to create a truly excellent book. *Whose Permission Are You Waiting For?* left me feeling inspired and empowered to take my next steps and celebrate the journey I've been on so far.

–Anne-Marie Maw | St. Agatha's Primary School, Brisbane, Australia

William D. Parker is more than just a friend of mine—he's a professional development provider, podcast host, leadership coach, and someone I proudly call "My Brother from Another Mother." Parker's genius shines as he masterfully blends personal stories, practical advice, and actionable strategies to guide educators on a journey of self-discovery, professional growth, and empowerment. From avoiding binary thinking to mastering consistency, monetizing your skills, and building systems, each chapter is a treasure trove of insights. His call to stop waiting for permission and embrace your passions is both a challenge and a gift, making this book a must-read for those who want to transform their dreams into reality.

–Dr. Don Parker | Author, Speaker, Educator, Chicago, Illinois

Each chapter feels like a valuable coaching session, guiding the reader through essential considerations when contemplating a change in professional path. From weighing income projections to recognizing the long-term rewards of your choices, Will encourages you to look beyond a limited set of alternatives. He offers real, actionable advice on how to leverage your talents, practical strategies for expanding your impact, and the mindset shifts that lead to lasting success. This book is a wonderful resource, suitable for professionals at any stage of their career. You'll find your best thinking as you walk alongside a wise friend through these pages.

– Donna L. Hayward | 2023 National Principal of the Year, Haddam-Killingworth High School, Higganum, Connecticut

Table of Contents

Foreword . . . . *xv*

Preface: *Will You Take a Walk with Me?* . . . . *xvii*

Chapter 1: *Understanding Your Pathways in Education and Why It Matters* 1
    A Little History of the Education Profession 4
    What about Other Models? 5
    Let's Wrap This Up 8
    Time for Reflection 9

Chapter 2: *Avoiding the Binary* 11
    Let's Apply This to Your Pathway 13
    An Example from My Odyssey Plan 17
    How Does This Apply to You? 18
    Let's Wrap This Up 20
    Time for Reflection 22

Chapter 3: *Curiosity + Inquiry = Discovery* 23
    Applying Complexity to Your Pathways 25
    Let's Be Curious 25
    What Happens with Inquiry? 27
    What Are You Discovering? 28
    Where Are You Going? 30
    Time for Reflection 32

Chapter 4: *The Value of Consistency* 33
   Why Consistency? 34
   Moving the Needle 37
   One Rake at a Time 38
   Time for Reflection 41

Chapter 5: *Will It Fly? Trial and Error in Taking Action* 43
   Why Beta Testing Works 44
   Will Your Idea "Fly"? 44
   Applying "Will It Fly?" 46
   What about You? 49
   Time for Reflection 50

Chapter 6: *Whose Permission Are You Waiting For?* 51
   What If the Biggest Barrier is Yourself? 53
   Just Do It 54
   Avoiding Fool's Gold 56
   Time for Reflection 57

Chapter 7: *Let's Talk About Money* 59
   Salaried Options 60
   Location Concern 61
   Part-Time or Gig Work 62
   Content Creation 63
   Training and Presenting 64
   Becoming Your Own Boss 65
   Staying True to Your Core Values 67
   Time for Reflection 67

Chapter 8: *Building Systems That Produce Outcomes You Want* . . 69
   Why Systems Matter 70
   Your Calendar Reflects Your Priorities 71
   Seeking Assistance 73

TABLE OF CONTENTS

    Online Tools 75
    Business To-Do's. 76
    Let's Wrap This Up 77
    Time for Reflection 78

Chapter 9: *Cycles of Reflection for Lifelong Learning and Growth* 81
    Cycles In Your Learning. 83
    Reflection on Goal Setting 84
    Life Score Assessment 85
    An Example of My Yearly Goals. 86
    How Does This Apply to Doing What You Love? 88
    What's Ahead of You? 88
    What If Goal Setting is Discouraging? 89
    Time for Reflection 90

Chapter 10: *The Value of Coaching and Why You Need One* 93
    My Early Mentors 99
    Let's Wrap This Up 100
    Time for Reflection 102

Chapter 11: *The Value of Masterminds for Collective Growth* . . . 103
    The Benefits of the Peloton Effect 107
    Intentional Accountability. 108
    You're Not Alone 109
    Shared Solutions 110
    Let's Wrap This Up 110
    Time for Reflection 111

Chapter 12: *Liturgies of Life That Shape Your Present and Future* **113**
   A Shell of Myself 115
   Your Mindset 116
   Your Nutrition 116
   Your Sleep 117
   Your Environment 118
   Your Movement 119
   Your Relationships 120
   Let's Wrap This Up 121
   Time for Reflection 122

Chapter 13: *Finding Your Greatest Joy Is Not What You May Think* **123**
   Doing What You Love 124
   What are Your Greatest Joys? 128
   Avoiding Imposter Syndrome 128
   Let's Wrap This Up 130
   Time for Reflection 130

Chapter 14: *How Mentoring Others Shapes You, Too* **133**
   The Do's of Mentoring 134
   The Don'ts of Mentoring 136
   Doing the Next Thing 136
   The Chapter You're In 137
   Let Mentors Shape You 138
   Letting Go 138
   Time for Reflection 140

Chapter 15: *Imagination Multiplied to Work and Life* **141**
   Thinking Bigger than You've Imagined Before 142
   Imagine the Possibilities 144

TABLE OF CONTENTS

    A Case Study in Imagination Multiplied 145
    Impacts on Individuals and Systems 147
    Your Limits Invite Collaboration 149
    A Word of Caution 150
    Time for Reflection 151

Chapter 16: *Backward Mapping for Reaching Goals.* **153**
    Beginning with the End in Mind 154
    Studying Abroad Example 159
    The Joy in the Journey 161
    Time for Reflection 162

Chapter 17: *Scaling Your Influence* **165**
    Let's Wrap This Up 171
    Time for Reflection 173

Chapter 18: *Pitching Yourself.* **175**
    Let's Wrap This Up 179
    Time for Reflection 180

Chapter 19: *Showcasing Your Profile* **181**
    Résumé Sample 182
    A Few Résumé Pointers 185
    Letters of Endorsement 185
    A Website or Webpage 186
    LinkedIn or Other Social Media 187
    Promo Video 188
    Let's Wrap This Up 188
    Time for Reflection 189

Chapter 20: *Applying Cycles for All of Life* **191**
    Let's Wrap This Up 196
    Time for Reflection 197

Conclusion: *A Final Conversation Walking Together* 199

References 207

Acknowledgments 211

About the Author 213

More from ConnectEDD Publishing 215

Foreword

Normally, when I find myself answering the same questions again and again, I realize that it's time for me to write another book. This book is in response to the many conversations I've had with educators over the past few years asking me questions like: *How do I know what is next for me in my current position or career? Should I choose option A or option B? When do you know it's time to do something new?*

None of the responses in the following pages are intended to give the false impression that I know the answers to all these questions. Instead, I invite readers to explore stories, examples, and practices that have helped me and others navigate the challenges of being an educator.

Because we work in a caring profession, caring professionals seem to consistently be coming up against the tension of supporting others while also making sure they are finding deep satisfaction in their own work and lives. I don't believe the choice between those two alternatives is a binary one. Read ahead if you are someone who wants a deeper understanding of your own motivations, practical advice for navigating a career as an educator, and helpful strategies for acting. Most importantly, read ahead to be reminded that doing what you love does not require anyone else to give you permission. Begin here for a journey of doing what you love!

–William D. Parker, February 2025

PREFACE

Will You Take a Walk with Me?

At the time of writing, I am enjoying the remoteness and quietness of a few days away at a friend's farmhouse in northeastern Oklahoma. For thirty years, my friend's family has built memories on these rocky trails, open fields, and rambling streams. For many years, this quiet place has also been a refuge for many of their friends like me, especially when I need time away for writing.

Ten years ago, I visited here for the first time, and an old quarter horse named Boon greeted me by the barn each morning with an invitation to brush his long mane. Sometimes he allowed me a slow ride around the pasture or into the fields.

Over the years, we have brought our children to this farm to explore the woods and creeks. The last time I came here, I came alone after my father died. My friends gave me a weekend here to reflect, pray, and find solace in the quietness. This time I'm visiting only nine months later, grieving my mother's death. Like so many stories of lifetime partners, her decline came shortly after his.

My father was a hard-working man with a blue-collar background, a joy for whistling while he worked, and a love for being a husband of almost sixty years, father to six, and grandad to more than a dozen grandchildren and great-grandchildren.

WHOSE PERMISSION ARE YOU WAITING FOR?

My mother was a poet, a young woman who begrudgingly agreed to having children and then spent her life joyfully pouring into them. In her older years, she found time to write again and to walk the woods by my childhood home. She was always a guide and counsel to others.

Nothing can prepare you for saying goodbye to your parents. A part of your life that has always been there is suddenly removed. There is a vacancy without a name—an emptiness that is as mysterious as trying to describe the color of the wind.

When my dad died, it was unexpected news. Although he had suffered for many years from the results of a stroke, he had found his slower stride in daily doings at the house. My brother, Sam, had come to make dinner for my parents when my dad appeared lethargic and without appetite. After dinner, Dad asked to lie on the couch. Sam took his blood pressure and was alarmed. "Dad, I think we should take you to the hospital."

"Why would I want to do that?" my dad asked. "If this is my time to go, I'd rather not spend it in the cold hallways or rooms of a hospital. I'd rather rest right here in my own house."

My brother called an ambulance, and he and my mother waited by his side. Moments before the paramedics arrived, Dad began to fade. They all held hands.

"You know we love you," they said.

"You know I love you, too," he whispered.

And then he was gone.

Mom's death was more gradual, with time for the family to gather for goodbyes. I was traveling at the time, coming home from an education conference in Alabama, when I received a text from my older brother, Jesse, who told me that Mom was in the hospital and failing. I called him back, and my mother was still able to talk. My siblings, nephews, and nieces who had made it there in time read to her from one of her favorite scripture passages, Psalm 91: "He that dwelleth in the secret place of the Most High will abide under the shadow of the

PREFACE

Almighty. I will say of the Lord, He is my refuge and my fortress. My God in whom I trust."

My mother passed away a few days before Thanksgiving. We gathered for her funeral, and then we stayed together for a large family reunion and meal. It was such a comfort to be surrounded by those who loved her—the people she had spent a lifetime loving and nurturing to become reflections of her influence.

A few weeks after her passing, a friend asked me if I had chosen a word for the new year ahead. I don't normally choose a word of the year, but I decided to try, and I chose the word *seed* in honor of my mother.

"William, this body is just a shell," she'd say, patting her chest and looking me in the eyes. "Each day in life, we are planting into others in meaningful ways. Our influence doesn't stop in this lifetime. Even in death, our influence continues spreading in those whom we've touched."

She was right, you know. The memories others will have of you, their acts of kindness, their trust and faith—like a beautiful plant or tree—keep growing like vines or branches, stretching and blossoming with new bounty long after your time is complete.

You may be wondering why I'm beginning this book by inviting you to take a walk like this down memory lane. Here's why: I spend most of my days working with educators—people like you who care deeply about serving students, teachers, and communities. They are hardworking, talented, passionate people who pour themselves into others and spend their time serving others. But sadly, you are not always allowed to be served. You also need time for walks and sharing what's on your heart and mind.

When I spend time with people like you, I often hear similar struggles—stories of complex situations requiring wisdom and insight. Sometimes, I hear tales of heart-breaking failures or disappointments. At other times, I hear joyful celebrations of happy moments.

I'm discovering some similarities in the questions people ask me. I am also finding myself sharing some of the same stories, suggestions,

WHOSE PERMISSION ARE YOU WAITING FOR?

or ideas with each one. Much of the time, I hear an unspoken sentiment in the questions they ask. I hear a yearning to be reminded that what they are doing matters. Often, I see educators wrestling with wanting to do the work they love most without the barriers erected through systems they cannot control.

To be clear: Many educators I work with are providing amazing service to their communities and producing exemplary outcomes. At the same time, many of these same high-performing educators seem to be waiting for someone's permission to do what they love most. Perhaps you can relate.

> Many educators I work with are providing amazing service to their communities and producing exemplary outcomes. At the same time, many of these same high-performing educators seem to be waiting for someone's permission to do what they love most.

- You know your days are limited, and you want to make the most impact.
- How do you know the work you are doing is making an impact?
- How do you give yourself permission to do the things you know will bring the most joy or satisfaction in your work and life?
- How do you know you are planting seeds toward a future you will be glad to embrace?

If you picked up this book, it's my guess that you could use a good walk to unpack your own thoughts as an educator and as a person. I know this is true for educators reaching out to me. Just a few days ago, I "walked" with three different educators through some phone calls:

PREFACE

Wendy's walk: The first call involved a young teacher. Wendy was interviewing for an opening as an assistant principal at a public high school. She had a solid track record of success in teaching and coaching. However, she was feeling overwhelmed with the unknowns involved in the committee interview she was anticipating. She wanted help thinking through the possible questions she may be answering. What should she do?

Ted's walk: The second call came from a principal, Ted, from a charter school in a large city. Ted felt trapped. The unrealistic expectations of his sponsoring organization were competing with the interests of the school board guiding his day-to-day operations. In short, he was being asked to choose opposing priorities between separate groups—both to whom he is accountable. What should he do?

Marsha's walk: The third call came from a central office director named Marsha from a religious private school system. This organization was searching for a new visionary leader, and Marsha felt unable to move forward on important initiatives with an emotionally absent leader at the top of the organization. Without a strong leader at the helm, my friend was trying to decide how to move forward when teachers, staff, and leaders were not unified around a shared vision. What should she do?

For Wendy, Ted, and Marsha, the scenarios may have been different, but the basic questions were the same:
What do I do next?
How do I know I'm making the right decision?
What pros and cons do I need to consider?
If you are an educator, I imagine that you can relate to some parts of the walks of Wendy, Ted, and Marsha. You want to see growth and improvement in your personal life and school community. You are skilled in your work and are gaining valuable experience in the ups and

downs of education. Like many others, you grapple with the "What next?" question in your decision making, growth, or goal setting.

Will You Walk with Me?

When I was young, I would often walk the gravel road near my home. For more than a mile, I saw nothing but nature—no power lines or homes—just pastures with grazing cows, and as I walked along, the trees on either side of the road touched branches, forming a long tunnel for the pathway ahead.

We may not have a peaceful road where you and I can walk and talk, but perhaps you're also a curious wanderer like me—someone who finds themselves facing hard choices or uncharted pathways—the traveler who asks, "What should I do next in this pathway I'm on?"

Welcome to an opportunity to walk together and explore some possible solutions. I invite you to take a journey with me through the steps I've taken to carve a path in education and beyond. This book is about exploring the options available when facing hard decisions. It is also a call to break traditional molds and give yourself permission to explore what you love rather than wait for someone else to open the doors for you. Here's a sneak peek of what we will learn together:

In Chapter 1, I discuss traditional pathways—how many of us are trained to follow predictable routes in our careers—but there are other models offering multiple pathways, and you can apply your own skill set to the education options that fit you best.

Chapter 2 is about avoiding the binary. I've been a teacher, principal, executive director, and business owner, and I'll share personal examples of how to think in pathways, creating flexible plans rather than ones dictated by others.

In Chapter 3, we explore how curiosity plus inquiry equals discovery. I'll show you how decision making becomes clearer when you take time to explore, interview, and investigate different opportunities.

PREFACE

Chapter 4 covers commitment to consistency. If you want to grow, it requires intentional action every week or day. I talk about platform building and how the power of consistent action and results lead to truly mastering something—so you can start building momentum.

In Chapter 5, I draw from entrepreneurial ideas to explain why testing your ideas through trial and error, beta testing, and learning by doing are critical to success. You'll see how applying cycles of learning can lead to breakthroughs.

Chapter 6 is the heart of the book: Whose permission are you waiting for? Stop waiting for permission from others. Study, experiment, and create your own platforms. Don't wait for someone to tell you what to do next.

Chapter 7 focuses on monetizing your skills. Not every passion leads to profit, but I'll help you think about options like salaried positions, gig work, books, podcasts, and even full-time ownership of your talents.

Chapter 8 is all about building systems. If you want to support the work you love, you need a strategy. I'll guide you through setting up calendars, online tools, bookkeeping, and even choosing between small business options.

In Chapter 9, I emphasize consistent reflection. I share how I assess my life's score with yearly, monthly, and weekly reflections, and how breaking down goals into daily tasks helps me stay on track.

Chapter 10 dives into the value of coaching. Drawing from Michael Bungay Stanier's seven key coaching questions (Stanier, 2016), I talk about the importance of being coached and coaching others—and how we can grow by being on both sides of that relationship.

Chapter 11 explores the value of masterminds. Collaboration with others for ongoing learning, reflection, and problem solving is a powerful tool, and I'll share how you can incorporate this into your journey.

In Chapter 12, we look at rituals and liturgy. Our habits, nutrition, environment, and relationships shape who we are. I'll explain how these elements, along with the universal right to rest, are critical to your long-term success and well-being.

Chapter 13 focuses on not losing yourself. Through stories and experiences, I remind you to find joy in your work and to stay grounded in what truly brings you satisfaction.

Chapter 14 is about mentoring others. I share why it's important to pass the torch and help others learn to do the next thing, avoiding the trap of being the "advice monster."

In Chapter 15, I challenge you to multiply your imagination. Push yourself to think bigger than what you originally planned. Avoid a scarcity mindset, and apply this approach to your goals for one year, five years, or even ten years, and see what happens.

Chapter 16 introduces backward mapping. By thinking from a destination point and planning backward, I've been able to achieve major milestones, from leaving traditional pathways to starting my own business. I'll show you how to apply this method to your own goals.

In Chapter 17, I share lessons on learning to scale your influence. Growth happens when we build up others. I encourage you to leave every room better than you found it, lifting others up, and collaborating to achieve more together.

Chapter 18 may feel uncomfortable, but it's necessary: pitching yourself. Learn to show your best side to others in interviews and first-time interactions. I'll walk you through how to memorize your intro and outro and present yourself as a consultant or confidant.

Chapter 19 is about showcasing your profile. Your résumé, endorsements, and presentations should be updated regularly. I'll help you think about how to showcase yourself effectively, whether that's through LinkedIn, a website, or even a promo video.

Finally, in Chapter 20, I talk about applying cycles of life. The same principles of reflection and inquiry can be applied to relationships, future planning, spiritual growth, and even travel. You'll see how these cycles have worked in my life and how they can work in yours.

PREFACE

In the conclusion, I wrap up with a personal reflection on "keeping the light on" for you.

If you are like me, you may pick chapters that resonate with where you are, but I want to encourage you to read this book from start to end. Each concept builds on the one before it.

Ultimately, I hope this book serves as a guide for your own adventure and encourages you to take action toward doing what you love. Whatever the time or season, perhaps it is time to give yourself permission to explore your boundaries, consider your options, and make the most of each day. This is why I'm inviting you to take a walk with me.

Let's Wrap This Up

This morning, I walked the fields on my friend's farm, minus the horse who passed away a few years ago. Even in his absence, the sun shone with golden light across the tops of the sagebrush like when we used to ride together. Bug, the farmhouse dog, ran up to me with his tail wagging, and then he pranced ahead on the trail that leads into the hilly woods behind the house. With gloved hands, I stooped to remove branches that had fallen along the path since the last time I walked here.

As I plodded up the hill, I came to a precipice where I could see the fields, ponds, and farmhouse below me. Winter had made the trees leafless. They stood tall like sentinels on the hill across the valley, lining their way along a rambling creek—their gray trunks slanted against brown, leaf-covered forest floors.

Moments like these give me pause to reflect on the most important questions in life. They remind me of the question I hear often from friends and colleagues: "How do I make decisions that lead me to experiences and outcomes that are fulfilling, flourishing, or rewarding?"

The answer to that question requires a much deeper and existential answer than this book addresses. However, I will say that doing what

WHOSE PERMISSION ARE YOU WAITING FOR?

you love begins with a willingness to take a step back from the moment you are in by looking to the past, examining the present, and considering the future.

If you're willing to take that kind of walk with me, welcome to the journey ahead.

CHAPTER 1

Understanding Your Pathways in Education and Why It Matters

Everyone has their own stories that lead them to the pathways they walk. Let me tell you a brief version of mine.

As a boy, my walk to the school bus stop was down a long, graveled drive near where my family lived in west Tennessee. At the bottom of the hill was a pile of dirt left from when the county sent a road grader to level out the rocks and dirt.

One morning, my brothers and I decided to play "king of the hill" before the bus came. My mom had packed our sack lunches, and for some reason I had taken the bag of chocolate oatmeal cookies out and placed it in my back pocket.

By the time the bus arrived, we were covered in dirt. After climbing aboard, we headed to school, down the gravel road, across the highway, and past fields of corn, soybeans, or grazing cattle.

I shuffled in my seat until I remembered my cookies. When I pulled out the bag, what was left was a mass of smashed brown crumbs. This didn't stop me, however, from opening it and trying to place as much of the mess into my mouth as I could salvage from the ruins. This was Will Parker at six years old.

Springville School provided my education from kindergarten through 8th grade. My teachers lived in the same community, and most of them had earned education degrees and been certified to teach as Tennessee-licensed educators. I played basketball at that school. I learned piano from a teacher who taught part-time at the school. My classmates all knew each other well, as there were only thirty-five other students my age.

By the time I started high school, I was a teenager with feathered hair and an affinity for skating rinks and music by Kenny Rogers. When I started high school, we were bused to the county school, where all the K–8 community schools consolidated their students into a high school with 1,800 other students.

Even though I had grown up on a farm and lived near a small town, the experience was pretty disorienting. Being surrounded by so many new people caused me in many ways to become self-protective and wary. A few months later, my world turned upside down when my dad reenlisted in the Navy, and we moved to New York and later to Virginia. The culture shock of these moves taught me a lot about the world. To summarize that era of my life, by the time I graduated, I had attended three different high schools.

Going to college for me was a difficult decision. Neither of my parents had been to college, and I was too embarrassed to tell my school counselor I didn't know how to apply. We were back in Tennessee in the fall after graduation when I injured my wrist in an accident while chopping wood. This accident gave me some time to think and pray about my future. During some long walks behind the farmhouse back in Tennessee, I began to consider my pathways: Should I go to work like many of my peers? Should I consider postgraduate education like college or career-tech? I was an average student, but I also enjoyed learning, especially reading and writing.

UNDERSTANDING YOUR PATHWAYS

After an entire semester out of school, I decided to travel for a weekend visit to an out-of-state university, and afterward, I applied and was accepted. I declared English education as my major because English was the subject I enjoyed most in school, and I thought education would give me a practical pathway. When I entered the teaching field, I followed a similar pathway to the teachers who had educated me:

- I taught classes within my certification areas.
- I sponsored clubs and took on extra duties for small stipends.
- I taught summer school or worked odd part-time jobs to supplement my income.
- I married my college sweetheart, who also became a math teacher, and when we became parents, I began working on a graduate degree in education leadership.
- After eleven years in the classroom, I became an assistant principal, a role I held for nine years before becoming a high school principal.

Where am I going with this brief life history? Along the pathways I took on this journey, most of the decisions I made came without a lot of research or understanding of the options. I was a product of my environment and culture. I explored the interests right in front of me. I would talk to others who had been down the path ahead of me. I would consider what the possibilities were in front of me, and I would explore or apply to see if I would be accepted. If a door opened up that appeared to be a good option, I would normally accept it and continue down the pathway.

Each of us has a different story, and you may or may not have some things in common with the pathways I chose. Interestingly, when I have learned the stories of other educators, I have discovered their pathways forward have been very similar to other educators once they became teachers. We worked hard to learn curriculum. We searched for new ways to understand student learning. We took on more responsibility over time. When newer pathways opened, we earned the qualifications necessary and stepped through open doors that seemed like the right fit. I'm not sure at what point I began to ask questions:

- Why are the traditional pathways in education so similar across the United States?
- Why is it that the structures of traditional K–12 schools have changed very little in the past century and that the career pathways for young educators have also changed very little?
- Why do most educators I know make so much less compared to others with the same level of education?
- Are there other options that exist for someone on this pathway? If so, what are they?

Before I move forward, let me be clear: I love the career pathway of teaching and learning. As a classroom teacher, I found no greater joy than seeing the light in a student's eyes when they were discovering new information. As a school administrator, I found no greater joy than supporting teachers having those same experiences. The joys also came with struggles and challenges, but the growth I have experienced as an educator is something that has shaped me and changed me in profoundly positive ways.

Having said that, I also want to take an honest look at why the pathways in education have also created systems requiring educators to think outside the box.

A Little History of the Education Profession

An average teacher enters the profession expecting that they will develop as a classroom teacher with a salary schedule that incrementally increases from year to year. Most U.S. school districts provide a salary schedule that provides small increases for 25 to 30 years. Sadly, most educators also earn significantly less than others with bachelor's degrees.

According to the Economic Policy Institute, "On average, teachers earned 73.6 cents for every dollar that other professionals made in 2022. This is much less than the 93.9 cents on the dollar they made in 1996" (Allegretto, 2023). This income disparity often motivates an educator to take on extra work or consider other roles in the school that may pay more than teaching. For some educators, this may include an administrative role. If an educator chooses one of those leadership roles, they may later be interested in district-level leadership roles filled by directors, assistant superintendents, or superintendents.

The challenge with this traditional model is the limited pathway options inherently available for individuals who may have interests, gifts, or talents that do not match these inherited trajectories.

When I talk to educators who feel stuck in their current role, I like to offer them some perspective. First of all, the system itself has been built with certain limitations in place. This is not necessarily negative. Student learning is the number one goal for schools, and our current systems are designed with the idea of providing as many students access to learning as possible.

For the educator, however, we are not necessarily trained to consider where those systems take us in our career pathways.

What about Other Models?

In contrast to traditional U.S. education career pathways, consider options for education majors in Singapore. University students there are asked to consider three pathways as they begin their careers:

1. Teaching to become a master teacher, coach, advisor, and mentor.

2. Teaching to become a researcher, college-level instructor, and developer of resources for curriculum and practice.
3. Teaching with the goal of school administration, with an understanding of organizational management, budgeting, and human resources (Boey, 201).

What options would U.S. educators have if the pathways gave newcomers the ability to consider options from the beginning, like master teaching, curriculum development, or organizational leadership?

Although some districts across the United States have begun introducing newer options like instructional coaches or behavior specialists, the point is this: Most educators look at their growth in the profession from the perspective of pathways already defined for them by tradition and limited availability.

I want to bring this perspective to mind because, whenever I talk to educators who are making difficult decisions about their current roles or considering future options, many times their options are determined by the pathway they are already walking.

Whether the traditional options work well for you, however, is irrelevant to what I suggest you consider next when thinking about doing what you love in education. Instead, I ask educators to permit themselves to consider the following questions:

1. What is it that you want to do?
2. Are you limiting yourself to the traditional options available or thinking outside the box?

These questions are core to understanding what kind of work, activity, or outcomes bring you the most joy while serving others. Exploring these questions are more important than job title or career pathway.

Patrick Lencioni in his book, *The 6 Geniuses of Work*, asserts that when people work within the areas of competency that bring them the most satisfaction, they are more likely to commit to sustainable and fulfilling work experiences. Likewise, others benefit from being around you when you are doing work that brings you great satisfaction (Lencioni, 2022).

Let me be clear. I am not suggesting that you cannot or do not find fulfillment and satisfaction in the pathways available in most traditional school structures. Instead, I am asking you to be aware that those pathways are not the only available trajectories for someone considering their potential to do what they love in education. The point is to keep in mind that the education landscape in front of you is as varied as you are willing to explore and imagine.

> The point is to keep in mind that the education landscape in front of you is as varied as you are willing to explore and imagine.

If you are interested in developing a mindset for being aware of the various pathways in front of you as well as cultivating an interest in exploring some options you may never have imagined, you must first recognize the pathway you are currently traveling.

A few years ago, I picked up *48 Days to the Work You Love* by Dan Miller. I was exploring for myself whether education was still the best pathway for me. To my surprise, the more I reflected, the more I realized that education was the field for me. I also realized, however, that education has many options, including the following:

- Teaching in public school settings
- Teaching in private school settings
- Instructional coaching
- Administration
- International school options
- Education resources and supports

- Curriculum
- Professional development

When I realized that the pathway I was traveling had multiple options available, I was able to consider my current pathway with the perspective that other potentially beneficial ones existed too.

Let's Wrap This Up

As a little boy, I rarely thought about how I ended up in a rural west Tennessee farming community, catching a bus along a gravel road each morning. I just walked the pathway in front of me, wrestled with my brothers while waiting for the bus, and then fished out my broken cookies afterward for the long drive ahead.

In some ways, the freedom of not choosing my pathway gave me a relatively normal childhood experience. In other ways, I knew very little about how much my inherited pathways marked the possible options that lay ahead of me. When I arrived at school each morning, however, my teachers welcomed me, with dirty clothes, cookie crumbs, and all.

Each of us is the beneficiary of the care someone provided us—even when we were unaware of all the pathways in front of us. With a growing awareness of the world, however, we now have some choices in what happens next.

These ideas on pathways lead me to the importance of avoiding the binary—something we'll cover in the next chapter. Before we go into more exploration, here are a few questions to reflect on when considering your pathways in education.

Time for Reflection

1. When you think about the pathway you are currently following, are your choices based on what is most familiar, or have you considered possibilities outside the box of your current pathway?
2. In what ways might your skills and talents be applied in other schools or other industry settings?
3. Think ahead to three years, five years, or ten years from now. What do you imagine yourself doing that would bring you the greatest satisfaction in your work?
4. Who are some educators or non-educators serving in ways that you see as bringing great value? Can you see yourself doing something similar in the future?

CHAPTER 2

Avoiding the Binary

When I was a language arts teacher, my students and I read Homer's epic poem *The Odyssey*. The story follows the journey of the Greek hero Odysseus, who, after the Trojan War, begins a long journey home by ship. The tales of intrigue, temptation, danger, sorceresses, and monsters weave a powerful tale for a hero who does not arrive home until twenty years after his journey begins.

My favorite scene in *The Odyssey* is when Odysseus arrives home and disguises himself as a shepherd. He wants to see if his wife has remained faithful (although he has not been faithful to her—a contradiction of morals typical to ancient literature), and he is aware that other men are competing for his place in his absence.

When Odysseus, still disguised as the shepherd, challenges the other men to a contest with his old bow and arrows, none of them can bend the bow. In a moment of heightened drama (cue the suspenseful music), he pulls the bow and shoots an arrow through the openings in a row of axe heads lined up across a room, hitting the target on the other side. Then he pulls down the cloak covering his head, declares his return, and begins shooting arrows into his enemies until he has single-handedly conquered the intruders and regained his wife and rightful place as ruler of his island.

These stories were first passed down through oral tradition almost three thousand years ago, before becoming poetry read by the Greeks; however, the power of the narrative still captivates audiences today.

As a fan of *The Odyssey*, I was intrigued when I came across the term *Odyssey planning* in the book *Designing Your Life: How to Build a Well-Lived, Joyful Life* by Bill Burnett and Dave Evans (2016). The authors, both design engineering professors at Stanford University, use the term as a way to discourage making choices as either A or B options. Instead, they encourage readers to think of decision making more like A, B, C, or D options.

This concept means to redesign decision making as a way to avoid the binary. Most of us like to think we need to choose between going left or going right or choosing between one direction or the other. The complexities of hard decisions, however, normally provide us with multiple choices.

Marketing agencies have discovered that consumers are more likely to purchase when they are only given two or three options. The average person likes these limited choices because they require less complexity and consideration for a relatively simple decision. However, when it comes to making *difficult* decisions, it is beneficial to realize you have more than A or B to consider.

When Burnett and Evans wrote their book, they were teaching design engineering courses at Stanford University, where they consistently met high-achieving students who were stumped about what to do with their degrees after graduation. As a result, Burnett and Evans developed an elective course for students to apply the same principles of design engineering to their own career pathway choices.

One of their first suggestions was to eliminate binary thinking and replace either/or options with at least three possible trajectories. I began applying this kind of thinking to my pathway in decision making before I discovered their book, but since they coined the phrase *Odyssey planning*, I have since begun using it as well. Although applying this principle looks different for each person, let me share an example of how I used it in my pathway planning.

As a teacher, I loved teaching writing. When I was serving as a high school administrator, I realized the pathway options for me were limited—especially any that gave me more time to write. I could write on the side as a hobby, but my income depended on my role as a principal. At the same time, if I wanted to promote or significantly increase my earnings, I could consider moving into district leadership or becoming a superintendent of schools.

Instead, I began to think about what other options better fit what I loved to do while I served as a building-level administrator. For me, that included writing, and I began a blog for school leaders. Eventually, I committed to writing a piece of content each week and posting it on my own website.

Later, I decided to transition my blogging into podcasting. After two years of this content creation, I compiled the works into my first book for principals. Then, two years later, Solution Tree Press reached out to me to inquire about publishing a book with them.

At the same time, I was presenting regularly for my state principal's association and was offered the role of executive director with the association. This was an unexpected pathway to consider. After much prayer, consideration, and wrestling with pros and cons, I took the position, knowing it fit well with the skills and talents I possessed. I also knew it was important for me to consider how that pathway matched potential options for me in the next five to ten years.

Let's Apply This to Your Pathway

If you are an educator, you are already on a pathway. It may be the pathway of teaching, school administration, or research. Whatever pathway you've chosen, you may have ideas of the future ahead of you, or you may be trying to consider your next steps.

What would happen if you considered those options with three or more potential outcomes? My guess is, if you are like most others, you have a difficult time thinking in pathways. Instead, you may be thinking, "Well, I can do what I'm doing, or I could choose a second option."

I want to invite you to avoid the binary and give yourself permission to imagine and plan out at least three potential pathways ahead of you. In this chapter, I will show how I have done this in my current pathway work, but the same can apply for someone just beginning in their education career. To illustrate this point further, let me tell the story of two teachers, Thomas and Annie.

Thomas's Story

Thomas was an 8th grade science teacher whose certifications made him capable of teaching advanced subject areas like biology, chemistry, or physics. Thomas, however, loved middle school. Physical science courses had become his passion, not so much because he loved the curriculum as much as he loved watching his students' faces light up when they made discoveries or participated in science projects that brought theory to life.

As a young teacher, Thomas spent his first few years just learning the ropes of classroom management, lesson planning, and grading practices while trying to keep himself from drowning in the new responsibilities. Thomas looked up to his department chair, a twenty-year education veteran who was a master at planning her curriculum and project-based instruction. One day, she asked Thomas if he would help her during his planning period by compiling an inventory of supplies teachers had available for labs and projects.

Thomas loved spreadsheets, so he volunteered to create a database they could use from year to year to track inventory. His department chair was thrilled to have Thomas's assistance. In the following year, Thomas took over tracking inventory for the team.

In year six of his teaching career, Thomas became curious about what it might be like to teach some upper-level courses or even become a department chair. To teach more advanced classes, however, his school would require him to move to a high school setting. Plus, his current middle school department chair wasn't retiring anytime soon.

He began to study the salary schedules available on the district website, and he discovered that the most significant salary increases come from administrator roles. After much thought and deliberation, he enrolled in a graduate program in education leadership. After earning his master's degree, Thomas began looking for openings.

In the following few years, Thomas experienced the new roles of dean and then assistant principal at the high school level. This pathway created moments he enjoyed, including coaching teachers and advising struggling students. At the same time, his role as a disciplinarian and supervisor of after-school activities often proved exhausting.

Later, Thomas applied for a job as principal at a middle school. This role brought him into new territories like budgeting and operational management—something he found himself enjoying. The best part of the job was being back at the middle school level with students and teachers who shared many of the traits he first loved as an educator.

The hardest part of his job, however, was managing accountability for teachers or staff who were not performing to standard or whose behavior required reprimands or dismissals. By this time, Thomas was in the latter half of his education career. He planned to stay in school administration and remain in his current role. Pursuing a district-level position or superintendency did not appeal to him. Overall, he found he enjoyed his work even with the complexities and challenges of the position.

WHOSE PERMISSION ARE YOU WAITING FOR?

Annie's Story

Now, let's consider Annie. From her early days as an elementary school teacher, she enjoyed the discovery and innovation involved in lesson planning and student learning. Her classroom was a place of creativity, using arts and technology to create engaging learning experiences. Because she also loved technology and its power to influence learning, Annie spent a lot of time exploring digital tools to enhance literacy.

A few years into her teaching career, she teamed up with a friend of hers who was talented in programming, and together they developed an innovative learning app that brought stories to life through gamification. This journey resulted in lots of invitations to present to other educators through workshops and conferences, where she taught about digital literacy, sharing her insights and inspiring others to explore the potential of technology in their classrooms.

Eventually, her work caught the attention of district leadership, and she found herself invited to lead in a new position providing support and instruction for teachers using digital tools for literacy across the entire district.

As Annie stepped into the second half of her education career, she realized she was finding the same joy in instructing and supporting teachers that she had found in teaching students. Her opportunities for advancement in the district, however, seemed limited to her current position.

One summer, she decided to partner with a firm that showed interest in monetizing the app she had created for enhancing digital literacy. Over the next few years, Annie experienced the joys of watching this partnership grow into newer business opportunities. She opted for an early retirement so that she could launch a consulting business that would bring her lessons, digital tools, and professional development to other districts.

Running a business was not easy, and Annie had to learn the downsides of tasks like calculating business taxes and negotiating contracts.

Overall, she was glad she chose the pathway she was on, and she tried to dedicate most of her time to teaching others, where she found the most joy in her work.

Perspective Check

The journeys of Thomas and Annie demonstrate two educators who are both passionate and talented. Their stories also illustrate the difference between a more traditional pathway in education and a more nontraditional one. It is important to say that we cannot be the judge of whether Thomas or Annie chose a better pathway than the other. I would say they both chose the pathways best for each of them. Most importantly, the stories of Thomas and Annie illustrate what happens when you avoid the binary and consider multiple pathway options.

An Example from My Odyssey Plan

In the first half of my career, I followed a very traditional pathway from teaching to school administration. In the second half of my career, I decided to move into a support role for education leaders by going to work for our state's association for secondary school administrators. At the same time, I had also become an author and professional development provider on the side.

I have a superintendent certification as well, but I was not sure if I wanted to continue supporting leaders from the outside or move back into a district leadership role. One summer break, I took time to write out the potential pathways in front of me. I was still exploring where my current pathway may be taking me and what other options might exist in the years ahead. I decided to create what I'll refer to as my own Odyssey plan. Here's a brief example of what mine looked like at the time:

- Option A: Executive director at a state association
- Option B: District leadership role
- Option C: Education consulting
- Option D: Combined executive director and part-time consultant

For each area, I considered the following:

- Income projections
- Potential retirement options
- Pros of doing satisfying work in each role
- Cons of doing frustrating work in each role
- Barriers or limitations inherent to the positions
- Potential for growth or expansion in each role
- Long-term potential results and an end-game when I reach my late 60s or early 70s

Within each of the potential pathways, I created very practical steps, ongoing education, geographical locations, and salary options that may be involved in pursuing each pathway.

Creating an Odyssey plan allowed me to investigate each option through research, conversations, books, podcasts, or interviews with people in these fields. These investigations often led me to open doors or opportunities to learn more. As a result, I began developing a hybrid approach by building skillsets that worked within each area while looking for the best opportunities that would help me reach my goals.

How Does This Apply to You?

Perhaps you are content with your present position or pathway. If so, congratulations. My guess is that people reading this book are looking for permission to do what they love, whether in the context of where they are or where they want to be. In either case, when I'm coaching other educators, here are some questions I encourage them to consider for at least three pathways:

- **Option A:** In the position you currently hold, what is the logical trajectory if you stay where you are?
- **Option B:** What is another possible transition within your field that may include a promotion or bring you more satisfaction in work?
- **Option C:** What is an option you would pursue if fear of failure or loss could be removed from the equation?

The benefit of this kind of thought process is that it allows you to build potential outcomes within each category. Then you can begin to add additional pathways and possibilities, allowing you to map out actions or steps necessary for those pathways. As you build options, you also begin to see what potential open doors may be available in each one.

In my journey, creating optional pathways helped me recognize when an opportunity in front of me was a potential match or open door for one of the options in my pathway planning. At the time of this book, I have authored three books and launched a full-time education consulting business—work that is both satisfying and surpasses the initial goals and targets I originally set. I have been able to hire my first executive assistant. The work has scaled to the point where I am now including other consultants who work for me as independent contractors.

My story is not a guarantee that pathway planning works for everyone; however, it is an example of what has worked for me, and it may be something that can help you too.

Let's Wrap This Up

The Disney+ series of the Percy Jackson stories are based on the bestselling books by Rick Riordan, following the journey of a young boy and his friends. Percy struggles with dyslexia and attention deficit disorder, and he does not realize until later in the first book that he is a demi-god. It is a modern version of another Greek Odyssey-style journey.

Percy and his friends set off on a quest, and throughout their adventure, they run into dangers, threats, and monsters and eventually find themselves facing Hades, the god of the underworld. Children and adults love these stories because they combine the elements of mythology, fantasy, and modern characters with conflicts, adventures, heartaches, and hope.

We all love a good story, but we would probably be bored if characters in a story were traveling along with no hard choices. Most of us would stop paying attention if the plot of a story failed to include internal or external conflict. Heroes are often faced with difficult decisions that require both courage and sacrifice. They seldom choose between just two alternatives. Most often, heroes face a complexity of situations and make choices that lead them to the unexpected.

The stories that feature characters like Odysseus and Percy Jackson have something else in common, however. Each one has an author, and the author controls the outcome for their characters.

In your story, the stakes are much higher than a work of fiction. You don't have a hired editor who can suggest potential changes to the script. You don't have the luxury of repeating days you already lived. You also don't have the benefit of positioning yourself outside your own story to analyze or choose your future.

At the risk of sounding too philosophical, I would like to make a value statement that helps me think clearly when considering hard decisions. In most situations, people have control over their decisions and are given both the autonomy and the responsibility to make important choices. At the same time, most people realize that they are part of a universal experience with meaning and influence beyond their control. Farmers experience this every day when they control conditions for soil, seeds, and fertilizer. Yet they cannot control the miracle of a seed sprouting or conditions of drought or flooding.

> In most situations, people have control over their decisions and are given both the autonomy and the responsibility to make important choices.

As a real person—as opposed fictional characters like Odysseus or Percy Jackson—you have choices:

1. You can recognize the current pathway you are on and discern whether it allows you to pursue options or possibilities you haven't previously considered.
2. You can predict potential options and pathways that complement your talents, skills, or qualifications while considering which ones do not match your values.
3. You can avoid the pitfall of believing that decisions are normally between option A or option B. Most of the time options C, D, or E also exist.

I want to ask you to consider how avoiding the binary in your decision making may be an important place to start when making difficult decisions about your pathway. We will talk about how to see the pathway more clearly in the next chapter, but for now, I invite you to reflect on the above with the following questions.

Time for Reflection

1. What is the current position you have and its logical trajectory as you move along this pathway?
2. What is another possible transition within your field that may include a promotion or bring you more satisfaction?
3. If you could pursue an option where fear of failure or fear of loss could be removed from the equation, what would that look like for you?
4. Write out potential pathways you may need to consider in your own work or life pathways.

CHAPTER 3

Curiosity + Inquiry = Discovery

When John and Molly Chester founded Apricot Lane Farms in 2011, they took on the daunting task of rehabilitating and redesigning more than two hundred acres of land that previous farming attempts had abandoned. The soil, which had once boasted orchards, was now dead. An irrigation pond was empty. With the help of an older farmer, Alan York, who became their mentor, they envisioned a traditional-style farm with a variety of fruit trees and a blend of farm animals, including ducks, chickens, pigs, sheep, and cows.

The task of rehabilitating the soil was their number one job. With the help of an investor and the enthusiasm of a team of like-minded young people interested in traditional farming, they began the hard work of installing a robust composting system, refilling the irrigation pond, and introducing animals back to the farm.

John Chester, who is also a filmmaker, captured the story of their journey through the documentary *The Biggest Little Farm* (2018), which chronicles the first seven years of the farm's new life—its trials, failures, discoveries—and eventually how it flourished.

WHOSE PERMISSION ARE YOU WAITING FOR?

When Alan York advised them on the design and vision for traditional farming, he encouraged them to focus on diversity and complexity. By composting, introducing animal life, and growing cover crops, the Chesters would be reintroducing an ecosystem that would eventually sustain fruit trees, egg production, and animal husbandry.

These benefits, however, would not come immediately or without their costs. In the first few years, the Chesters experienced enormous development as cover crops grew and animals grazed, but they faced many setbacks, including wildlife killing their ducks and chickens, snails devouring the leaves of orchard trees, sick pigs and sheep, and birds destroying their fruit. With each setback, the Chesters had to reevaluate and decide what part of the farm could be productive while responding to the parts that were being damaged.

The inspiring part of their story was their undying optimism and their purposeful reflection in the face of diversity. Alan became sick and could no longer help them. Their mother pig, Emma, became deathly ill. Coyotes were killing chickens by the dozens. Gophers destroyed the root systems of fruit trees. The Chesters, however, continued monitoring and adjusting, nourishing the soil with compost and water, and allowing the crops and animals to work together in creating a healthier ecosystem.

As John's voice narrated in his documentary of the farm, "Coexistences can't be forced. It's a delicate, patient dance." Eventually, the systems created among the soil, trees, and animals reach a tipping point. Chickens began eating garden pests, natural predators like owls began killing gophers, ladybugs arrived to protect plants from aphids, and hawks protected the trees from fruit-eating birds.

Today, Apricot Lane Farms is a bountiful traditional farm that sells produce throughout northern California. Tours of the farm are sold out each season. John and Molly Chester's dreams of traditional farming continue today with constant care, problem solving, and intentionality in maintaining a healthy ecosystem.

Applying Complexity to Your Pathways

In addition to avoiding the binary, I would like to explore why embracing complexity, looking for lessons, and building a broader perspective helps in decision making. Whenever I talk to educators who are navigating their pathways in serving schools, most of them agree that the first few years of any new position come with a lot of anxiety and uncertainty.

> Embracing complexity, looking for lessons, and building a broader perspective helps in decision making.

Like a good farmer, an educator knows they must invest a lot of time in the foundations of building relationships, creating workable systems, understanding their unique roles and responsibilities, and managing the outcomes of their students or teammates. Over time, you begin to realize what is working and what is not working. With enough time, most educators who become veterans learn how to anticipate changes, analyze choices, and act accordingly.

When it comes to determining your potential pathways as a career educator, you may also be curious about pursuing other positions, or you may be interested in how you can apply the skills you've learned in other settings or industries. Whatever the case may be for you, realize that the same curiosity, inquiry, and discovery we encourage in learning cycles work for our career cycles as well.

Let's Be Curious

For instance, if you are considering options in your career pathway, where might you begin? Look around. Even in your own school setting, you are surrounded by people, resources, and supports that require a complexity of services for schools to exist:

WHOSE PERMISSION ARE YOU WAITING FOR?

- Accounts payable
- Administration
- Activities
- Archiving records
- Athletics
- Book purchases
- Building maintenance
- Cleaning services
- Clubs
- Counseling
- Curriculum
- Customer service (front desk personnel)
- Food and nutrition services
- Graduation announcements and apparel
- Human resources
- Individual education plans
- Infrastructure development
- Language learner supports
- Legal services
- Library services
- Nurses
- Online services
- Paraprofessional support
- Psychologists
- Speech-language pathologists
- School security
- Societies
- Special services support
- Sports apparel
- Student information systems
- Student or staff photography services
- Teaching

- Technology support
- Textbooks
- Therapy
- Transportation
- Trauma-informed care
- Tutoring
- Website design
- Yearbook sales

For each one of those areas, schools invest in personnel, products, expertise, or training to ensure the complexity of these services all come together to support student learning. Curious people notice the work others are doing outside of their own area of expertise and take an additional step: inquiry.

What Happens with Inquiry

When I was a young teacher, I began to realize someday I wanted to step into school administration. I would ask my administrators a lot of questions about their pathway into their roles. After many of these conversations, I began to see some similarities in the responses I was receiving, and the feedback helped me imagine some of the obstacles, challenges, and opportunities ahead of me if I became a school leader.

In addition, I also began to look around the rest of the school and ask other questions: What is the role of the school registrar? Who manages payroll for our salary deposits? These weren't necessarily areas I would be responsible for managing if I became an administrator, but I realized these support personnel were an integral part of the whole picture. One day, I took my planning period to visit our district's central office. I met with the staff member there who was responsible for payroll. She showed me her own system for managing personnel records and processing. She was also responsible for ongoing invoicing services.

I didn't know much about these systems as a classroom teacher, but my curiosity led me to inquire.

I mentioned the book by Bill Burnett and Dale Evans, *Designing Your Life*. In their design-thinking model, they recommend anyone interested in a potential career option spend time inviting others to coffee or for a short conversation to ask questions. These kinds of inquiry sessions allow you to pick someone else's brain and learn more about their skills and expertise.

One example of this is found in a fellow educator, Nick Davies, who serves as an assistant principal in Vancouver, Washington. Two years ago, Nick began a year-long journey of inviting a different person to meet with him each week via Zoom. The list was based on people who were doing interesting work he admired and wanted to know more about. During that time, he conducted more than fifty interviews that he cataloged each week on his LinkedIn page.

Nick also began inviting fellow educators to meet with him on Zoom to share ideas and problem solve. He applied these lessons with the students, teachers, and families in his own school community. His collaboration and hard work did not go unnoticed. At the end of 2023, the Washington Principal Association recognized his work as an education leader by awarding him the 2023 Assistant Principal of the Year.

Nick's curiosity led him to inquiry, and his inquiry has given him access to information for his own work and insights into the work of others he would have never gained otherwise.

What Are You Discovering?

Finally, curiosity that leads to inquiry will often lead to discovery. Whenever I work with educators who are considering changes, I encourage them to write down possible pathway options (as I mentioned last chapter). The value of identifying options is to give you tangible ways to dig for more information.

CURIOSITY + INQUIRY = DISCOVERY

Let's unpack one example. If someone is considering changing from their current teaching role, they might consider options like taking on another grade or subject area, instructional coaching, working on a degree in another education field, transitioning to college teaching, or even something as dramatic as starting their own education consulting business.

> **Curiosity that leads to inquiry will often lead to discovery.**

Let's assume they decided to write down at least three of these options. Underneath each one, they write out the questions they may have about those positions. Here are some examples:

- Who might they know, or who might they find through a search online to find out more about what is involved in that field?
- Are there any available articles or books that would give them insights into each of those options?
- What would the salary ranges or potential income options be?
- Would the options require additional training, education, or certification?
- Is there someone or someplace they could visit to find out more?
- What times and/or dates could they place on their calendar (e.g., once a week, twice a month, once a month) to pursue these inquiries?

Finding the answers to these questions opens up new ideas and possibilities. Sometimes, this kind of exploration introduces you to new people who see your interest and point you to another source who could help you in your search. Along the way, you begin to identify the pathways, and some of these can become open doors or possible opportunities for you.

WHOSE PERMISSION ARE YOU WAITING FOR?

Over the course of my work as an educator I have often asked, "I wonder how that works?" The beauty of the age we live in is that we can find out almost anything if we ask the right questions. For instance, in 2012 I wondered how someone creates a website. I was interested in starting one where I could write blog posts about lessons I was learning in education leadership. I came across the work of Michael Hyatt, an author who also had a successful blog and website, and he had created a twenty-minute YouTube video explaining how to start a website using WordPress (Hyatt, 2013).

Over winter break, I took time to watch the video and apply the lessons. In 2013, I launched my website at williamdparker.com. My mother and a few friends were my first readers. Over time, that website began to see more traffic. After three years of adding content to it each week, I decided to begin a podcast. I didn't know how to begin a podcast, so I found a YouTube video by Pat Flynn, who had built a six-part series, originally accessed in 2016 with an updated version available as of 2021 (Flynn, 2021). I watched all six videos over a winter break and then posted my first episode on williamdparker.com.

Fast forward to today, and the episodes on *Principal Matters: The School Leader's Podcast* have been downloaded more than 1.4 million times with more than 400 episodes available to date.

Writing online content eventually resulted in my decision to write books. I didn't know how to write a book, but I bet you can figure out what I did next, can't you? Curiosity, inquiry, and discovery are the same cycles we encourage in classroom learning. How can you apply them to your own pursuits and interests?

Where Are You Going?

Let's come back to the story about the Chesters and their farm. Early on, Alan York told the Chesters that diversity and complexity in the ecosystem of their farm would eventually lead to simplicity. Alan cautioned them, though, that "simple does not mean easy."

By the seventh year of the farm, Alan's words became reality. The return of a healthy cover crop meant rains were captured and stored in the farm's aquifer system instead of lost in run-off. The bounty of fruit trees brought back pollinating bees. The ranging animals added natural fertilizer to the soil with their droppings.

When I first watched the documentary *The Biggest Little Farm*, I was skeptical of the Chesters' ambitions. But as the story unfolded, I was inspired by their commitment to the culture of their farm—their dedication to the foundational principles of cultivating healthy soil and introducing cycles of nourishment and rehabilitating farming practices. I was also struck by their reflective leadership.

Many times, they faced situations where they were unsure how to find short-term or long-term solutions. For instance, when gophers were destroying the root systems of their fruit trees, it seemed impossible to get rid of these pests. As John Chester explains in the documentary, he began to "take a step back and watch."

And observation was followed by creativity. He decided to install owl nests around the farm, and soon these natural predators were killing enough gophers to protect the root systems and save the trees. Over and over, this became the pattern: a commitment to their principles of traditional farming while walking, observing, thinking, and problem solving.

These same principles work in other areas of life as well. When you

> When you give yourself permission to embrace the complexity of your environment, eventually you begin to see the patterns, possibilities, and opportunities in front of you.

give yourself permission to embrace the complexity of your environment, eventually you begin to see the patterns, possibilities, and opportunities in front of you.

These discoveries do not mean life or decisions become simple, but they can become easier. Once you've committed to this cycle, then you're ready for what's next.

Time for Reflection

1. What are the areas within your own school experience that you realize you have never explored? Make a short list of resources, supports, technologies, or positions you realize you've not investigated before.
2. As you look at your current skills and gifts, in what other subjects or positions may those same talents be applied that would bring you joy in your work?
3. Who is someone's work you admire? Set up a conversation by phone, video chat, or in-person over coffee, and ask them what they love about their work and what lessons they've learned to gain expertise.
4. Consider where you are today, and ask yourself whether your moments of satisfaction outweigh your more difficult ones. If not, what changes might you need to make to find more satisfaction here, or do other opportunities exist where you could find more joy in your skills and talents?

CHAPTER 4

The Value of Consistency

Years ago, I took my son Jack hiking in a state park in Arkansas. When he drifted off to sleep, I lay awake reading a book I had brought along, *Platform: Get Noticed in a Noisy World* by Michael Hyatt (2012). I was surprised to learn that most content creators, like bloggers or podcasters, give up on their content creation after one year of commitment. Dedicated creators will often make it three years before dropping out. People who persevere to the fifth year, however, see a shift in momentum that often pushes them into exponential growth.

The idea makes sense if you compare Hyatt's analysis to the law of averages or to the advice investment experts give us about long-term savings. The longer someone commits to developing anything, the more likely they are to gain exponential growth over time. We know this is not always true if the investments are not wise ones.

For instance, most of us have heard stories of pyramid schemes that bankrupt individuals. Or we hear about athletes who persevere in a sport only to find themselves unable to reach the next level due to the limits of their own abilities compared to the small percentage of elite athletes allowed to play at professional levels.

In education, opportunities are expansive, but the outcomes are not guaranteed. On average, however, the longer someone commits themselves to the mastery of a craft, the better the likelihood that they will find more satisfaction in their work, and the more opportunities they may have to use their skills in various applications.

Being a part of a system, however, that touches communities at every level may also mean finding it difficult to set yourself apart in the ways you want to leverage those skills or talents. If you're curious, inquisitive, and discovering ways you want to expand your opportunities in the field of education, then what can you do to reach the next level in doing work you love? I'd like to suggest one word that separates high-achieving individuals from others: *consistency*.

Why Consistency?

In another bestselling book, *Atomic Habits: An Easy & Proven Way to Build Good Habits and Break Bad Ones* by James Clear (2018), the author explains that the small actions you take each day, not just the motivation you have, will result in long-term growth and benefits. We know this advice is common sense, but we do not always apply it to the areas where we want to grow as educators or as human beings.

More than twelve years ago, I considered building my platform as an educator, and I committed. I began creating content to share with others about my experiences as an educator and leader. I knew I only had time for small actions. I decided that writing 500–800 words a week about a lesson learned that week was a doable task. The biggest decision I made, however, was to create this pattern of committed sharing for the next five years, because I wanted to see what would happen over time if I pushed beyond the average commitment other content creators were making.

THE VALUE OF CONSISTENCY

Each Wednesday morning, I shared a post on my website and emailed the link out to friends who had subscribed. Over time, the traffic grew as well as the number of subscriptions. The growth was modest, but my commitment stayed the same: one post a week, each week, each year. As my influence grew, so did my ability to compile my content into larger works as I did by writing books and creating presentations and courses for educators. Doing good work often leads to invitations to do more good work. I collected endorsements from those whom I was helping. I took risks by inviting listeners to coach or group sessions.

Through trial and error, I practiced lessons with audiences to see which ones seemed to have the most impact. I explored, discussed, and interviewed experts. I listened to podcasts and audiobooks and attended conferences. Most importantly, each week, I wrote the next post or recorded the next podcast episode. Whether it was weeks or months before I had another invitation to present my content, I knew each week I could move one step toward more momentum in helping others through consistency.

Eventually, my work caught the attention of my state principal association, and I was invited to join their team in supporting middle-level and secondary principals across my state. Even as I began this new work, I kept writing or recording one piece of content each week, each year.

Fast forward to today, and I now have enough momentum and invitations to say yes to supporting educators as my full-time work. When I announced I was launching a full-time consulting business coaching leaders, facilitating academies for educators, and speaking at conferences and schools, some of my friends asked me how I could replace my income as an educator so quickly.

The short answer is that it took me ten years to figure it out. Another answer is that I have been consistent. Each week, I have been creating content and sharing lessons with others every Wednesday for years. Like good gardening or farming, noticing small lessons in the complexities, honing skills over years of labor, relying on others for help along the way, and trusting God for what was not in my control had all borne good fruit.

Consistency works in other areas of our lives. Want a good routine for sleeping? Set a time each day when you're committed to shutting down your phone, wrapping up conversations, and reading in bed before lights out. Want a better workout routine? Try setting out your clothes or workout shoes for the next morning so you're not sleepily searching for them the next day.

Even as a father with four young children, I learned that if I at least tried to maintain a routine around bedtimes and sleep for our kids and myself, the chances were better that we successfully made it through most nights with better sleep. Yes, sickness, bad dreams, worry, and bad weather sometimes interrupt the best-made schedules, but the commitment to following a routine helps you beat the law of averages over time if the goal is a lifestyle of good rest. These examples of rest and exercise are just that: examples.

These same principles apply to any area where we may want to see growth or changes: a new certification or degree, exercise goals, nutrition improvement, reading aspirations, vacation planning, income management, relationship building, or spiritual growth—all of these may be affected by the habits we build and the consistency toward implementation.

So, what are the habits you wish you were practicing most often? Or, in other words, what is the life you wish you were living that would bring you the most joy and satisfaction? If your habits and actions over time are shaping you toward that end, then which ones can you consistently practice to build the mental, emotional, and tactical muscle for reaching those outcomes?

THE VALUE OF CONSISTENCY

Moving the Needle

When I drive a car, I pay attention to the speed limit. When I accelerate or decelerate, I can see the needle on the speedometer move up or down. As an educator, I often found myself at the end of the day asking the same question: Did I make a difference today in moving in the direction we have said is most important at this school? If I could answer that question with a tangible example from my day, I asked, What is one action I can take to move the needle in the direction of our most important goals before I leave today?

Sometimes this meant sending a short text to someone who helped a student or fellow teacher that day and telling them thank you. At other times, I composed a quick email to the staff highlighting a celebration or expressing gratitude for student achievement. Occasionally, I sent an email to parents with some reminders about ways the school was helping students or showcasing good news. I like to call these actions "moving the needle" in the direction you want to grow.

The same concept applies to your growth as an educator and human being. If you realize you need to move the needle in your goals and growth, you might decide to take a few minutes to do so in the following ways:

- Calling a friend to touch base and asking about an area they are celebrating or find challenging.
- Listening to a podcast during your commute home (or while making dinner) that motivates your growth as a leader.
- Listening to an audiobook that inspires or challenges your thinking.
- Texting a few friends to remind them that they are important to you and to wish them well.
- Saying a prayer for someone you're concerned about or asking for wisdom and perspective on your own challenges.

- Resting your mind or body by sitting quietly for a few minutes with your eyes closed, not listening to anything.
- Taking a quick walk outside to breathe fresh air and enjoy the feeling of movement.
- Inviting a friend or family member for a quick coffee or snack to enjoy reconnecting.
- Writing a positive social media post to spread good ideas and encourage constructive engagement.
- Jotting down a few ideas in your notebook, journal, phone, or writing projects.
- Reviewing your to-dos, goals, and calendar and choosing one area where you might take action in the next five minutes.

One Rake at a Time

When I was in college, I mowed a lot of yards to make extra money. In the fall, sometimes I raked leaves. One day, some friends and I were invited to clean a property that had about five acres of trees surrounding a beautiful home. When we arrived, I looked at the blanket of leaves surrounding us for as far as we could see.

"I don't think we can clear this property in one day with only rakes," I said to my friends.

An older buddy of mine looked at me and said, "Well, we won't get it done if we don't start, and that will only happen one rake at a time."

He began to rake, and the rest of us followed his lead. Throughout the day, we began suggesting more ways to speed up the process. We used a mower to help blow the leaves. We piled them onto long tarps and pulled them in big piles. We raked and raked, and at the end of the day, the property was clean.

Over the years, I have thought back to that story many times in my own work and pursuits. Many of us look at the pathways ahead of us or the goals we want to reach, and the sheer volume of tasks overwhelms us.

THE VALUE OF CONSISTENCY

Guess what? Feeling overwhelmed is a normal response to any big plans. What can we do to make progress?

Do the next thing.
Do it again and again.
Do it consistently.
Do it over time.

When you follow this pattern, you will eventually look back and realize that you've made a lot of progress. Eventually, small habits executed consistently over time will lead to outcomes that never seemed possible when you first started.

> Eventually, small habits executed consistently over time will lead to outcomes that never seemed possible when you first started.

Malcolm Gladwell's (2011) book *Outliers: The Story of Success* made famous the idea that when someone commits 10,000 hours to practicing a craft, they master the craft. The ideas that Gladwell shares have resulted in criticism from the authors of the research Gladwell quotes in his book. They clarify that practicing in the right ways over time can lead to mastery, and the amount of time is arbitrary, as we know different people have different levels of commitment or expertise (Skillicorn, 2016).

The ideas in Gladwell's stories, however, present a helpful lesson: People who find themselves highly skilled in their fields commit consistent time to develop, practice, and hone those skills over time. In some ways, I am simply repeating what you already know instinctively: small, consistent habits of excellence over time tend to produce exponential growth.

At the same time, as I work with very talented educators who are asking questions about what is next in their growth or roles in education, many of them already have dreams and desires about where they would like to exercise their skills in the years ahead.

They may have updated their résumés or explored options with research or direct conversations. They may already be exercising consistent habits toward new goals. Many of them tell me, however, that they feel frustrated at the lack of progress or movement they are experiencing. My response: What you are feeling is normal. You may decide over time that some pursuits are producing the outcomes you thought they would. It's OK to change direction or pivot in your pursuits—just as we talked about earlier in avoiding the binary.

Let me be clear about what I am *not* saying about consistency: I am not saying it is easy. The complexities involved in life and work require nuance in our thinking and applications.

Several months ago, I was having a conversation with a group of leaders in an online mastermind group I facilitate. We were talking about ways to improve student behaviors and outcomes. One of the participating leaders said, "Data on student performance is important, but what is more important when working with students is starting with the question, 'What do you value?' *Let your values guide the outcomes, instead of letting the outcomes guide the values.*"

This leader's response helped me remember what I am also not saying about consistency. I am not saying you should commit to actions that don't include your most important motivations.

Your actions, habits, and practices are important commitments to achieving outcomes. However, if your motivation toward that end is based on the outcome and not based on the values you hold most dearly, then your consistency is simply an exercise in achievement rather than meaning. In other words, do not lose yourself in the process of pursuing your goals and dreams.

I talk to many educators each week who are struggling with whether they are doing the right work or making a difference. Whether a person is achieving outcomes is not as important as whether those outcomes are meaningful ones.

Your health, faith, relationships, and service to others are the bedrock of who you are as a person, not simply your achievements. You are not a machine. You are a person. Whatever pathway you are on, you will never perfect that journey. Keep that perspective in mind, give yourself the grace you want others to give you, and apply consistency in your goals without losing yourself along the way.

> Whether a person is achieving outcomes is not as important as whether those outcomes are meaningful ones.

In the chapters ahead, we will continue exploring other ways to build momentum and take action, but at this point, I simply want to remind you that meaningful and long-lasting change normally takes time. Decide what actions and habits you can take consistently that match your values each day, each week, each month, and each year toward your goals. The prospect is not easy or quick, but most meaningful outcomes are not.

Time for Reflection

1. What is one action or goal you are considering for your own growth or journey in education that matches your most important values?
2. What daily, weekly, monthly, or yearly actions and habits are you taking to reach those goals?
3. What is one action you can take today to move the needle in the direction you want to go?
4. Take one action right now that helps you do the next thing toward one goal that matches your most important values.

CHAPTER 5

Will It Fly? Trial and Error in Taking Action

When Wilbur and Orville Wright built their first airplane, their ideas were informed from a vast number of sources. Having read the works of others who had attempted to understand the physics of flight, the Wright brothers combined their own mathematical calculations with the practical knowledge they had as bicycle builders and repairers.

They also employed a friend whose skill in engine repairs became crucial for combining the gliders they designed with a small engine for propelling the machine.

In a 2022 interview with David McCullough, who wrote the book *The Wright Brothers* (McCullough, 2015), the author explains that the brothers experienced their first flight in 1903, but it was not until 1908 that the world began to accept the possibility that flying was an actual possibility for humans.

How were two brothers from humble beginnings able to transform the world with their invention—a world convinced that man would never fly? They began by testing their theories, experiencing failures, relying on people they knew, risking their safety and reputation, and refining their practices as they proceeded.

Why Beta Testing Works

When I was a high school principal, I remember one semester when teachers began discussing the possibility of modifying our master schedule to add more remediation time. I gathered a group of interested teachers, and we started brainstorming potential scenarios and master schedule options.

After a few meetings, I asked them to create two different schedules to use as pilots, each embedding remediation time at different points during the day. We announced to the teaching staff and students that we would be running a mock schedule on Monday to test mediation according to schedule A. Then we gathered as a team to review the experiences, performance outcomes, and concerns from that pilot. Two weeks later, we ran schedule B and followed the same process of review.

By beta testing schedules A and B, we discovered which one we felt most comfortable with and decided to implement the new schedule in the following spring semester. Planning so far in advance offered several advantages: it allowed for teacher input, gave both teachers and students an opportunity to practice, provided feedback on a potential future schedule, and alleviated some anxiety associated with change by preparing well in advance for the next year's schedule.

Will Your Idea "Fly"?

Piloting ideas is a helpful way for educators to test something before implementation and can be applied to decision making and considering options for career changes or professional growth. For instance, when considering a new position, shadowing someone can offer insight into whether it's a suitable long-term role.

WILL IT FLY? TRIAL AND ERROR IN TAKING ACTION

At one point in my early years in education, curious about whether I should consider different career options, I took a day during one break to shadow a friend in the insurance industry. This experience was enlightening–although I ultimately decided education was the right fit for me.

Similarly, one summer, our career technology center offered training for teachers and principals, including tours of local industries, to connect school activities with future employment sectors for students. It was inspiring to learn about industries outside my own from workers, managers, and owners.

Experiences like these can open your eyes to potential connections in the work you are doing at school or expand the possibilities when thinking about your own pathway.

Whatever decision making you are currently facing, a good question to ask is, "Will it fly?" Are you raising awareness for a potential new project? Consider pitching it to a small group for feedback. Are you trying to determine whether you're making the right decision about student discipline? Share your thoughts with a trusted colleague. Are you thinking about a transition in your career or seeking a new position? Try it before you buy it.

Reading books about other professions can also be a helpful way to see how others' experiences may inform your decisions. For example, when I read Dave Ramsey's (2011) book *EntreLeadership: 20 Years of Practical Business Wisdom from the Trenches*, I discovered insights into defining key responsibility areas (KRAs) for employees, a concept I adapted for the non-instructional staff at my school and have continued using when I've hired others in my own education consulting business.

The "Will it fly?" philosophy is one I have borrowed from Pat Flynn (2016), author of the book *Will It Fly? How to Test Your Next Business Idea So You Don't Waste Your Time and Money*. In the book and throughout his podcast, *Smart Passive Income*, Flynn discusses testing business ideas with a sample audience to determine if it meets their needs and then reengineering the idea for future audiences or clients.

This is a strategy I encourage school leaders to apply by piloting ideas with small groups before full implementation. It is also a strategy that works when testing ideas in decision making and a helpful concept for thinking about your own pathway in education. In some ways, it allows individuals to test ideas or roles in a controlled manner, provides valuable insights, and reduces risks associated with change. In other ways, it compels you to experiment, to take calculated risks, and to refine your expectations while learning more about yourself in the process.

As you consider your own pathway, it's essential to navigate the uncertainties that come with change. Whether you're thinking about teaching a new subject, stepping into an administrative role, becoming a college professor, or beginning work as an education consultant, each possibility comes with its own set of unknowns.

Or, perhaps, you are simply trying to move forward on a decision within your present position that would increase growth outcomes for students. Either way, let me share how these ideas of "Will it fly?" applied to my own journey.

Applying "Will It Fly?"

When I was a language arts teacher, a colleague of mine moved from her role as a science teacher to assistant principal in a neighboring district. The school had an opening for an Advanced Placement English teacher, and she reached out to see if I was interested. In addition to asking lots of questions about the school, I took off early one day to go visit the school.

We walked the hallways, I met other teachers, and I was able to imagine whether I would be a good fit. Any time I have considered a move in positions, I have followed the same pattern to investigate or visit places in order to better understand "Will it fly?"

WILL IT FLY? TRIAL AND ERROR IN TAKING ACTION

Years later, when I began exploring the transition from working as a school principal to opportunities in presentations, trainings, and consultations, I quickly realized how little I knew about the professional experiences in many of those fields. Inspired by the concept of "Will it fly?" I initiated conversations with individuals involved in state principals' associations and national consulting companies.

I talked to education consultants and presenters at conferences and set up phone calls to explore what their work entailed. These interactions allowed me to gauge whether such a career pivot was feasible for me.

Another "Will it fly?" strategy I employed was writing my first book to see if published content could open more doors. Writing a book was challenging, but it honed my skills and, upon completion, provided a way to share my insights with others. This effort led to invitations to speak and to present on the book's content. Additionally, I used the money I earned from a few paid speaking opportunities to pay a videographer to capture my work, creating a promotional video for prospective clients to preview my approach and expertise.

As my commitment to content creation continued, I had to think of other ways to see if what I was doing was scalable. What else could I be doing to make this work grow?

I remember a conversation I had with education author Dr. Jen Schwanke, who also co-hosts my podcast with me. I was explaining to Jen how my work with podcasting and content creation was growing opportunities, but it was also becoming an expensive hobby. I was investing time and money into content creation, but the invitations to do consulting or speaking events were not adequately supplementing all those investments.

Jen's suggestion to me was to say, "Well, do something about that. Take a risk on offering a new training or creating a course others could purchase through your podcast audience."

WHOSE PERMISSION ARE YOU WAITING FOR?

Her nudge of encouragement motivated me to include a call-to-action statement in a future podcast episode, where I told listeners to reach out if they were interested in joining me and other leaders for some virtual professional development.

I began by offering a free online group for school leaders with a six-week commitment. Anyone who wanted to join me afterward for an ongoing mastermind could opt to do so. A group of twenty leaders joined me for weekly online meetings for six weeks. At the end of that time, I invited those interested to commit to ongoing paid membership for continued collaboration, focused learning, and guided problem solving. Six of them committed.

What began as a "Will it fly?" moment offering professional development eventually became a model that I have used for years now in replicating online offerings for leaders. Each year, I have been able to add more groups and leaders.

At the time of this writing, I am leading more than one hundred education leaders in monthly or bi-monthly Principal Matters Grow Academies, Impact Masterminds, or one-on-one coaching sessions. Along with occasional keynote invitations, I am leading at least twenty sessions a month during an average school year.

All these opportunities are the result of starting with one offering to see whether the idea would work. The versions of trainings I am offering today look very different than when I first began offering them, but learning what works and what doesn't work provides an opportunity to know what is the next best step to take.

> **Learning what works and what doesn't work provides an opportunity to know what is the next best step to take.**

What about You?

These steps were my way to test the waters, assessing what opportunities might arise from this new direction. How might this approach apply to your own exploration? Before committing to whatever pursuit you think is best, consider how you can test these ideas to ensure they're viable for you. Here are some suggestions:

- **List potential changes:** Identify changes, fields, positions, job titles, or locations you're interested in as a new career venture.
- **Identify challenges:** Where do you see obstacles for moving forward? How might someone else approach solving these?
- **Seek feedback:** Reach out to individuals in those fields for insights on their experiences, lessons learned, and advice they'd give to their younger selves.
- **Shadowing:** Ask a colleague, friend, or associate if you can shadow their work to determine if it matches your expectations.
- **Volunteer:** Engage in volunteer work related to your interest area. This can help build skills, content, and a supportive network.
- **Create samples:** Develop examples of your work, such as a book, video, podcast, YouTube channel, social media feed, workbook, or handout, to showcase your expertise.
- **Pilot ideas:** Invite a group to pilot ideas with you, such as mastermind meetings with peers to discuss and solve problems together.

These steps can help you test the waters before making significant career changes, reducing the risks involved and ensuring a smoother transition into new roles or fields.

Before you take a step that feels like a high-stakes risk, allow yourself the small steps of trial, error, assessment, refinement, and redoing.

When you do, you allow yourself to build new knowledge, experience, and wisdom for the road ahead.

Time for Reflection

1. When was the last time you walked through a reflective cycle about your practices? If you can't think of a time, place time for reflection on the calendar right now.
2. How would you assess your strengths and weaknesses as an educator, leader, spouse, parent, and so on?
3. What is the correlation between your self-awareness and your ability to help others?
4. How might your motivations become lessons to guide, coach, or help others with theirs?
5. What are the variables or options you have been considering as you think about an important decision ahead? Share those ideas with someone who has experiences that may inform whether you are on the right path.
6. As you consider taking an important step, what is one way you could beta test or run a trial of the idea to see how it works on a small scale first?
7. After trying a new idea, reflect on the outcomes: What worked that you would want to repeat? What would you discard moving forward? If successful, how is the experience or the outcome something that can be expanded and repeated on a larger scale?

CHAPTER 6

Whose Permission Are You Waiting For?

Last spring, I enjoyed a trip to Charlotte, North Carolina, where I worked with a group of assistant principals in a full-day training on the key responsibilities involved in school leadership. After we wrapped up the day, I drove three hours east and met a friend who lives near Asheville, North Carolina. We spent the next two days hiking the trails that led us through woods, across streams, and to mountain overlooks. One of my favorite spots was standing by a stream at the base of a waterfall. The falls bathed a river that ran amber with glistening specks of fool's gold. I needed to pause along my travels to take wonder in the small things. Doing what I love involves more than the work I do as an educator. It also means taking time to pause, breathe, and reflect.

You chose this book for a reason important to you. Even though I may not know your story, I suspect you want to experience the most from your work and life. Although some of the opportunities available to you happen outside your control, I want to remind you that just as many opportunities are within your control. Reaching out and taking time to experience them often begins with permitting yourself to do what you love.

Most educators I know, because of the systems we've inherited or the environments in which we have been shaped, are trained to follow some kind of structure or system designed by someone else. Let me be clear: honoring traditions, history, and reliable systems can have great value. We all benefit, for instance, from rules for road safety or systems that restrain violent behavior. In school structures of authority, we want people to understand the key responsibilities of self-governance in a way that honors those structures, because we want the best possible outcomes for our shared community.

At the same time, I've also discovered that sometimes people create barriers that don't necessarily exist anywhere but in their minds. For example, when I was in college, I was part of a leadership development team connected to a scholarship program for resident advisors. We were invited to participate in a ropes course. For whatever reason, ropes courses were popular in the 1990s. Many of them involved physically and intellectually challenging activities that were designed to help teams build trust and a deeper understanding of their work.

We were in a grassy area and separated into groups. Then we were told that we had to cross a large distance without ever touching the ground in that area. This was only possible by creating a human chain of arms, legs, and bodies—allowing one person to crawl over the space with the hope that the last person was great at long jumping.

For some reason, I remember creating in my mind additional restrictions that were never communicated by the instructor, like thinking we only go forward, not backward, in the game. When teammates suggested moving backward, I thought they were cheating. Afterward, when we were debriefing, I expressed my frustration with the boundaries that I *thought* we had crossed.

The instructor asked me, "Will, why do you think you created a boundary for yourself and for the team that didn't exist?"

At that moment, I realized something new about myself I've never forgotten: I tend to create barriers or boundaries that aren't communicated. Sometimes imagined boundaries are as powerful, or more powerful, than actual ones.

Let's apply this to your work in education. When I coach or collaborate with educators who tell me they would like to implement new initiatives but they see limitations with budgets or upper administration, these barriers may be real ones.

At the same time, they may also simply be perceived as barriers. These barriers may also be what I referred to in an earlier chapter as a false binary. What if there is another option available that does not require budget approvals or input from upper administration?

For example, an educator may want to start a book club for colleagues to grow in their own professional knowledge. The same educator could ask their principal for permission to purchase books and send around an invitation to other teachers—a reasonable approach. What if they are told no because the resources do not exist to support this request?

The same educator could encourage a group of colleagues to buy their own books and meet at a local restaurant for dinner once a month to discuss what they are learning. Perhaps the same educator could place a call-out on social media for anyone they know who wants to participate in the book study and then invite participants to join weekly or monthly conversations through Zoom—bringing their book and favorite beverage!

Have you ever created limitations for yourself that perhaps only exist in your mind?

What If the Biggest Barrier Is Yourself?

People normally have more than one option available when considering a step forward. At the same time, if you find that all your ideas or movements consistently require someone's approval, you are probably either creating imagined boundaries for yourself, or you are part of a work environment where someone is exercising significant control over the actions and decisions of colleagues and individuals.

I am not saying that existing structures are good or bad, but I am suggesting people create barriers that either do not exist or could be faced with a different mindset.

I must admit I am guilty of sometimes taking action without permission. "Ask forgiveness, not permission," as the saying goes. As a result, I have also been reprimanded when I've crossed boundaries. This practice has served me well in times when I need to be innovative or move quickly in situations, and other times, it has required me to circle back and take the heat when I've crossed the line that someone else did not appreciate.

Quick note: Please do not blame me if you decide to risk the same approach and receive correction or pushback. At the same time, I am asking you to give yourself permission to step outside your comfort zone.

Just Do It

When you consider your own dreams and aspirations for doing more of what you love, here's the question I'm asking you to consider: *Whose permission are you waiting for?*

When it comes to making decisions about your pathways, innovative planning, career choices, and possibilities for a future, what would happen if you began to approach your planning with the freedom to do what you want to do, not waiting for someone's permission to dream, innovate, or take action?

Let me give another example from my own work in taking risks. When I decided to create content for education leaders, I realized that many of the things that I was writing could also be placed in publications, posted to other blogs, or submitted for articles in education magazines. Sometimes I would reach out and inquire if these other publications were interested in my content, and sometimes they would say yes.

Other inquiries would give me no feedback or leads. I began to feel discouraged. I thought, "Why am I not seeing traction or finding others interested in what I'm sharing right now?"

Then I remembered: I did not need to wait for their permission to share content for free. Nor did I need anyone's permission to publish on my own. I discovered that content can be shared in a variety of ways, including on social media sites, on websites like LinkedIn, in email exchanges, via email subscriptions, or by self-publishing.

This same attitude has served me well in other prospects. Self-publishing my first book led to an invitation from two reputable publishing companies competing for the opportunity to publish my second book with them.

Each week, for more than a decade, I have shared a new piece of content—a podcast episode or blog post—on my website and social media channels. This work happened while I was leading a school, continued when I became an executive director for Oklahoma's secondary principal association, and has continued in the full-time work I'm currently doing as an education consultant.

When no invitations are coming for a presentation or workshop, I don't ask permission to keep writing and sharing. When book sales dwindle to zero in a given month, I don't ask permission to keep writing and sharing. When algorithms change Google searches and cut my podcast listening audience in half, I don't ask permission to keep writing and sharing.

As a result, eventually, the consistency pays off. I'm doing what I love, and I do not need permission to do so. What is the action you want to take? What is the dream you have for engaging in the areas of life or work where you find the most joy?

Obstacles may exist toward that end, but they may also exist in your own thinking. Stop waiting for someone else's permission. Give yourself permission to do what you love.

Avoiding Fool's Gold

Know the lay of the land in whatever institutional setting you work. Having invited you to be generous with yourself, I want to add that many real boundaries exist for a reason. For instance, legal and ethical boundaries should be understood, respected, and not crossed.

Some institutions or organizations do not allow their employees to create content, post on websites, or speak at events without their prior permission. In many other instances, however, I believe we create those boundaries in our own minds first.

Just as my friend and I enjoyed hiking the trails in western North Carolina, we also knew that the sparkling flecks of gold in the streams we crossed were not real gold. Instead, what we were seeing were minerals called pyrite.

Pyrite's golden metallic sheen makes it look like gold, hence its well-known nickname of "fool's gold." Just because it was pyrite does not mean it was any less beautiful. At the same time, we did not fool ourselves into thinking we could gather up the pyrite to sell as gold.

My final point is this: Doing what you love must be connected to the core values you hold most dear, or you may be playing with fool's gold. I am asking you to consider thinking outside the normal boundaries you find yourself operating within and asking yourself what would happen if you moved toward the goals, actions, or habits that connect you with experiences that bring you joy. The value between fool's gold and real gold begins with knowing the difference.

Pursuing goals clearly connected to what you value most means saying no to false assumptions, removing self-erected barriers, and rejecting the imagined (or sometimes real) resistance of others to keep you from taking steps in the direction you know is necessary toward that end.

When you're ready to step out of your comfort zone, then you are ready to begin doing what you love.

> The value between fool's gold and real gold begins with knowing the difference.

Time for Reflection

1. What are some areas of growth you have dreamed about personally or professionally?
2. If you were to set new goals in your health, relationships, salary/income increases, or ability to give generously, what audacious goals would you want to set?
3. When you think about where you would like to be in work and life in one year, five years, and ten years, what outcomes would you hope to experience?
4. Now, be honest with yourself—whose permission are you waiting for to take steps toward the above ideas, dreams, and goals?
5. What might happen next if you gave yourself permission to take one action that would help you move in the direction you want to go?

CHAPTER 7

Let's Talk About Money

I have sat through hundreds of professional presentations in my years as an educator. Most seem to follow a typical framework: present a problem, explore solutions, inspire action, and walk away with a possible application.

Inevitably, many presenters like to endear themselves to educators by reminding them they did not choose this profession to make a lot of money. What many people don't think about is that most professional development presenters receive money (sometimes lots of it) to present to educators. I would like to say something to educators I do not think I have ever heard any presenter say before during professional development: *My fellow educator, I bet you would like to make more money.*

As we have explored in an earlier chapter, most educators are paid significantly less than other professionals with similar degrees or credentialed qualifications. If you desire to do work you love, you also deserve ample compensation. The good news is that you have options. Whether through a salaried position, a change of location, gig work, content creation, training others, or owning your own business, you can make more money doing what you love. Let's discuss these ideas in several categories.

Salaried Options

Most U.S. school structures create scales where teachers have an entry-level salary that incrementally increases over time. However, many educators have realized that their earnings are not keeping pace with inflation or matching the salaries of others with the same level of education and degrees, even though they understood the limitations of the profession.

With that in mind, the question becomes, "How do you leverage the skills you're learning to increase your options?" The answer will look different in every setting, community, city, and state. However, let me make some generalizations here:

1. It's important to look at the structures that already exist within your school and ask if there's any way you could benefit from the skills you have. For instance, many schools offer extra-duty pay for teachers who can sponsor programs, tutor students, or provide some after-school or before-school activity or care. This is why athletic coaches and activity sponsors often see extra-duty stipends in their contracts. If this doesn't exist within your system, I highly recommend looking for a school or organization that rewards extra work.

2. Some districts pay extra-duty stipends for roles such as department chairs, instructional coaches, and teacher mentors. These may be some other things to consider, as well as credit recovery programs and summer school programs. Some school systems offer evening or weekend classes for credit recovery or adult education, and many educators use their advanced degrees to work part-time for colleges or universities as adjunct professors.

Teachers of Advanced Placement courses have found employment through grants within their state departments of education, offering Advanced Placement summer workshops. Institutions like the College

Board have paid teachers in the summer to grade and mark Advanced Placement tests.

3. Many educators find employment in other education organizations like the College Board, test prep curriculum companies, and technology education companies, which consult or provide professional learning for schools. Search the internet for companies that support education, and you will discover hundreds of institutions and companies, both small and large, that employ former educators across the United States and the world.

4. Consider higher education. While K–12 education is my favorite setting, many educators transition to higher education as a part of their retirement planning, earning retirement income from their teaching careers while creating a second career. Some of these options depend on the state in which you reside and its unique retirement options.

Location Concerns

An educator's geographical boundaries may prohibit them from some of the opportunities I've mentioned. Fortunately, the internet has leveled the playing field for many who wish to live in a fixed location while working remotely and traveling when necessary.

For example, one national organization, the National Association of Secondary School Principals (NASSP), which services National Honor Society membership and Student Council membership, employs all its team members remotely even though their headquarters are based in Washington, D.C. Employees work from remote locations and gather for conferences, workshops, and services as needed. This is just one example of companies that operate this way.

In the school world, sometimes it requires courage to look beyond your boundaries. If your school doesn't provide you with a salaried position that can support your family, or with extra-duty stipends, you could request additional work within your district or look outside your location for a better fit for your skill sets that would reward you with an equivalent salary option or opportunity.

Not everyone has the same freedoms when it comes to movement because of family commitments, aging parents, young children, or marriages that require living where your partner or spouse may also have preferences and concerns. However, location is something to keep in mind in terms of opening more opportunities for yourself.

With the high demand for highly effective teachers and the small pool available, educators have the ability to move locations and find great work.

Part-Time or Gig Work

Although it is a sad commentary on public support for education, almost every educator I know also works outside of their teaching schedule to make ends meet. Some educators are privileged to be with a partner whose income supplements what they may lack in their salary. Other educators figure out how to do part-time work in addition to their full-time job.

I've mentioned some of these already, in terms of teachers who may work for the College Board to score tests, coaches who serve athletic teams, or educators who seek out sponsors. Gig work can come in many other forms, too. As a young teacher, I employed myself over the summer painting homes, mowing grass, filing records for corporate offices, as well as teaching summer school classes.

I know educators who repair roofs in the summers, service pools, or run dog-walking businesses. As I became a content creator, I began to understand ways to earn extra money through book publishing and keynote presentations—important gig work for me for many years. I also know educators who do gig work for ride-sharing companies and groceries or product deliveries before or after school hours.

Content Creation

Perhaps you're interested in becoming a content creator. Content creation can unfold in various ways, whether it's documenting the lessons you're learning as an educator and sharing them in other contexts or perhaps crafting a curriculum that could be replicated or duplicated in other settings. Some content creators engage audiences through podcast episodes, YouTube channels, or social media platforms.

Content creation is less about the creators themselves and more about meeting the needs of those interested in your content. A piece of advice I often give to content creators seeking to increase their influence sounds a bit cynical but here it is: Please remember, no one is thinking about you; they are thinking about themselves. If you're aiming to become a content creator, the key is to provide answers, solutions, or ideas that help others solve their challenges and questions.

> **If you're aiming to become a content creator, the key is to provide answers, solutions, or ideas that help others solve their challenges and questions.**

If content creation interests you, you might consider creating your own website. There are free options available through Google, and WordPress offers a paid website creation platform. Alternatively, you can hire someone to create a website for you where you could host all your content. Free platforms also exist through social media sites. Many educators use LinkedIn to share their ongoing content creation, while others use platforms like Facebook, Instagram, or Threads, and some are even turning to TikTok videos to share their insights. YouTube is another avenue for consistently showcasing content. Additionally, websites that allow you to upload video content and curriculum and share sales with creators are worth exploring for distributing your work. More about this in Chapter 19.

For those considering starting their own podcast, check out a series by Pat Flynn (2023) on how to create your own podcast could be beneficial. This YouTube series helped me embark on my content creation journey. Because learning is only fingertips away from your computers or phones, there are numerous ways to learn about maximizing and leveraging your content creation.

As the author George Couros told me in a 2024 interview for my podcast (Parker, 2024a), content creation should be about sharing meaningful lessons. If you're simply sharing content for the sake of sharing, then you are wasting your time and the time of others. Instead, focus on the meaningful lessons you are experiencing and discover ways to share those ideas and experiences with others. As a result, you benefit and so do others.

Training and Presenting

You may want to explore how to monetize your ability to train and present. Entering this market can be intimidating; however, a good starting point is to make people aware you have content to present. Offering your services for free is an excellent way to build a reputation and collect endorsements.

Over time, you can begin to inquire if organizations or groups have a budget for keynote presenters or closing speakers. You'd be surprised to find many do budget for individuals who can provide valuable learning in their areas of interest.

My first paid speaking and training opportunities occurred through my state's principal association. I am eternally grateful to individuals like Dr. Gracie Branch and Dr. Vicky Williams, executive directors at the time, who invited me to present at state principal association conferences in Oklahoma.

These platforms enabled me to connect with state associations across various states, many of whom began to request copies of my books or invite me to speak at their conferences.

Most educators receive information or feedback from organizations that provide training, such as the Association for Supervision and Curriculum Development (ASCD), the National Association of Elementary School Principals (NAESP), the NASSP National Association of Secondary School Principals (NASSP), and the Association for Middle Level Education (AMLE). These national groups offer ongoing conferences and content to educators across the United States.

If you take the time to study the websites of these organizations and look at their staff directories, you'll find individuals usually assigned as directors of content or professional learning. Reaching out to them with a free offering of your content, a book, or a piece of online content is a great way to build relationships and provide value, potentially leading to opportunities to be involved in their training.

Becoming Your Own Boss

Lastly, some educators are interested in consulting or creating enough work for themselves that could be a full-time endeavor, either as part of retirement or as a second career in educational services. When I considered starting my own consulting business, it was daunting, but a good friend encouraged me to register with my state for a Limited Liability Corporation (LLC) and receive a tax ID number. This allowed my company to be responsible for the content and any liability involved in training, protecting me in any unforeseen legal issues.

Owning your own business means you need to understand the processes of writing contracts, submitting proposals, sending service agreements, invoicing for services, and tracking your own quarterly tax payments. While the idea of business ownership isn't attractive to everyone, for others, the potential to scale and grow your income becomes an appealing opportunity to manage your own time, calendar, and schedule.

In all scenarios, one of the most crucial aspects to consider when thinking about monetizing your skills and talents is the value of your time. If you calculate your current hourly wage based on the salary you earn as an educator and the hours you work, you might be surprised at the value. The question then becomes, if you were to apply the same activities, knowledge, skill sets, talents, and knowledge toward providing valuable information to others, how much would you value your time?

All money-making is a value exchange. Sometimes, as educators, because we are not in for-profit businesses, we fail to ask ourselves the value of our time. However, if you were to consider that your time could be rewarded two or three times the amount you're currently making, you might begin to envision other ways to leverage your time.

Perhaps you did not pick up this book because you're interested in making more money. However, I rarely meet anyone who is not interested in having better control over their income, spending, and time. By understanding the options available to you within schools, different locations, gig work, content creation, training opportunities, or business ownership, you may find yourself considering options for your future that give you a greater return on the knowledge, expertise, and service you can provide as you grow in your work as an educator.

Staying True to Your Core Values

The question I like to ask about monetizing my skills is: How can I leverage the skills I've developed to maximize helping others while also increasing the amount of income available for the time I have available? Also, it is important that my work is prioritized in light of my faith, family, exercise, rest, and nutrition.

As I've mentioned before, you are not a machine. This chapter is to spark ideas toward alternatives so that you are not constantly thinking in the binary—between two choices. Income is an important part of work. At the same time, your quality of life is not directly connected to your income as much as it is to your mindset and commitments.

Time for Reflection

1. Do some math. Take your current annual income. Determine how many days a year you are actually working. Divide your annual income by that number. This number represents the monetary value of the time you dedicate to work. Please note that it does not represent your value as a person.
2. What kind of opportunities may be available for you to dedicate the same amount of time (or, in some cases, less time) and see an increased amount of income in exchange for your time? Give yourself permission to brainstorm and dream.
3. What skills, certifications, education, or additional learning would you need in order to pursue increased income?
4. What might be required for you to consider increasing the income in your salaried position, a different position, any gig work, your current location, content creation, or working for yourself?
5. Imagine if you were able to reach a new level in doing what you love. What outcomes would you hope for in one year, three years, and five years?

CHAPTER 8

Building Systems That Produce Outcomes You Want

A few months ago, I had the privilege to speak at a conference in Maryland. While I was there, I touched base with a retired educator and friend named Dave. Dave invited me to stay with him and his wife for a few days after the event and enjoy some sailing.

As a lifetime sailing enthusiast, my friend has taken many others on the water over the years. What a thrill it was to spend time in good conversation while aboard a beautiful 42-foot boat that glides across waves and water with the power of wind. At times, I helped Dave with the process of tacking and jibing (terms he had to teach me).

At one point, when the sailing was smooth and predictable, I moved to the bow (or front) of the boat. From there I could see the water cascading below me. The seas ahead stretched across the horizon and met the sky in an unending canvas of blue.

As wonderful as the experience was, this day did not happen without a system. Months and weeks in advance, Dave and I exchanged emails, texts, and phone calls. I scheduled my flight arrival and departure times to coincide with meeting him. My car rental was secured accordingly. We weighed the options of what to do in case of inclement weather. Dave was meticulous in his knowledge of navigation, maps, depths, and wind direction.

If you were planning a trip of your own, my guess is that you would pay close attention to when you scheduled your arrival and departure times. If you were flying, you would arrive early, you would pack with guidelines that limit fluids or other requirements of the Federal Aviation Administration. You would schedule a place for lodging. You would budget accordingly. Simple steps like that are helpful for a good traveling experience.

The same logic goes for everyday activities in schools: arrival and dismissal routines, lunchtime schedules, master scheduling, teacher absences, requests for transportation—all of these involve systems. When the systems are strong, understood by others, and followed consistently, then more efficiency and productivity may be experienced.

Now apply this to your own priorities in work and life. How are your systems supporting the outcomes that help you love the work you do?

Why Systems Matter

I'm sure you've heard the idea that if you still get the same outcome from the same system, perhaps you need to change the system. Pursuing work that you love requires more than motivation or passion; it also requires strategy. One of those strategies includes building systems that produce the outcomes that help you reach your goals. I want to

> Pursuing work that you love requires more than motivation or passion; it also requires strategy.

discuss some of the systems that have worked both in my educational background and in my consulting.

Mark Shellinger, the founder of the SAM Process, explains that most education leaders spend their time doing things that others could be doing instead of doing the things they're best at (National SAM Innovation Project, 2024). If you have been a classroom teacher, you know how frustrating it is to spend more time on compliance requests than on curriculum development or student instruction. If you have been an assistant principal or principal, you understand the frustrations of managing urgent requests that are not always tied to your priorities of teacher development or student learning.

If you take a step back from your own work, ask yourself: What are the outcomes that you're currently experiencing, and how have the systems that you created helped you reach those outcomes?

If you feel like you're not reaching the outcomes that are best suited to your skills and talents, or if you feel like you are ignoring the most important priorities and values of your work, the question may be centered on whether you've built the right systems to do the work that you're best suited to do.

Your Calendar Reflects Your Priorities

Each year, as a teacher, as a former school leader, and even in the work I do today, I have taken time to map out my entire year in advance. For classroom teaching, that meant using a syllabus and a curriculum map to know the direction that I needed to lead my students in order for them to reach the standards of learning and improvement they needed for each year.

As an education leader, I recognized the importance of teacher and student development and built my calendar in advance, including my observations, my evaluation schedules, my duty rosters, and my activity schedules in the summer before school began.

Today, I build my professional calendar in advance, sometimes two years in advance, in order to prioritize what is most important in the work. As a result, my calendar represents and reflects my priorities. I simply do not fill my calendar with what is urgent. Instead, I first prioritize what is important and then fit what is urgent inside that framework.

If you struggle with prioritizing your time and calendar, let me invite you to check out the interview with Mark Shellinger on my podcast, episode 414, from October 9, 2024 (Parker, 2024b), for a summary of ways to make better use of accountability, delegation, and "training others to use you as you want to be used."

The research behind scheduling your priorities is compelling. Mark was a teacher for seven years, a principal for ten, and a superintendent for ten more. External research confirms SAM leaders spend more time on instructional work, are happier, work a shorter day, are better liked by staff, and see improved learning results. More than 1,200 school leaders in 22 states do this reflective practice change process every day (National SAM Innovation Project, 2022). As Mark explains, the SAM process addresses challenges in prioritizing work, which is outlined in three key strategies:

1. Leaders scheduling their time to enhance effectiveness.
2. Engagement with a reflective partner to maintain focus and motivation.
3. Training individuals to interact with principals in a supportive manner.

These components encourage principals to allocate more time to instructional leadership, a practice that, according to Mark's research on more than five thousand principal practices, currently occupies only 22 percent of their time.

Mark encourages the importance of connecting with an accountability partner, with an emphasis on asking critical questions such as "What's next?" or "As a result of being in the classroom, what will you do now?" He underscores the value of reflective inquiry—asking important follow-up questions—in fostering improvement and supporting teacher development.

He also contends that managing people is *more* challenging than rocket science due to the inherent difficulty of facilitating change. He encourages educators to focus on targeted feedback, particularly the impact of celebrating success as a way to lessen the isolation educators often feel.

Finally, he advises educators on the importance of being accessible to one's team while also managing interruptions constructively. He suggests encouraging follow-up meetings as a way to maintain priorities, even in the face of emergencies (Parker, 2024b).

Seeking Assistance

In the book *Someday Is Not a Day in the Week* by Sam Horn (2019), the author shares an activity called the "Happiness Box." In the activity, you are invited to create a square and divide into four parts. Then you label the parts as follows:

Square 1: "What are you *doing* in your life that you *want to?*" (These are habits and patterns you are glad are happening in your work and life.)
Square 2: "What are you *not doing* in your life that you *want to?*" (These are habits or actions you wish you were doing more but are currently not doing consistently.)
Square 3: "What are you *doing* in your life you *don't want to?*" (These are habits or actions you would love to stop doing if you could.)
Square 4: "What are you *not doing* in your life and you *don't want to?* (These are habits or actions you have stopped doing—like smoking or being in a toxic relationship, for instance—and you are glad you are not doing them.)

WHOSE PERMISSION ARE YOU WAITING FOR?

I invite you to take a few minutes and write out responses to those questions. What you will discover is the correlation between Square 2 and Square 3. When you discover what you want to be doing, this begs the question: Could you eliminate an activity or train someone else to do something for you so that you have more time to do the things you really want to be doing?

This mindset has served me well in the classroom, schoolwide, and when consulting educators. For instance, as a classroom teacher, I spent a lot of time handing out materials and collecting materials back from students. One day, another teacher asked me why I wasn't training my students to do those activities for me. I had never even considered the option. Once I did, however, I suddenly had more time to do my other responsibilities in the classroom.

The same perspective helped me as a principal in training others on my staff, including students, to help me manage daily tasks, like announcements, answering phone calls, posting to social media—activities that once I had distributed them to others, freed me up to do more of what only I could do, such as advising teachers or observing classrooms.

In my podcast development, I was doing my own audio and newsletter editing for more than six years before it dawned on me that I could train someone else to do those tasks so that I could be free to interview more people or work on other projects only I could do. Eventually, I realized I could also have others help me with interviews as well. Dr. Jen Schwanke, who co-hosts my podcast, now interviews guests as well.

The correlation between what you want and what you don't want to do requires you to examine your habits and ask a simple question: Do I love the work I'm doing? If the answer is no, then you must examine what parts of the work might be delegated to someone else.

BUILDING SYSTEMS THAT PRODUCE OUTCOMES YOU WANT

Online Tools

By the time this book goes to print, more online tools will have been created than I would be able to list here. Instead of trying to create a comprehensive list of tools that save time, I will mention a few I currently use that might help you as well:

Grammarly: "An AI-powered writing assistant that helps correct grammar, punctuation, and style in real-time, which is great for efficient, error-free writing."

Calendly: "Streamlines the appointment scheduling process by allowing others to view your availability and book slots, eliminating the need for back-and-forth emails."

Canva: "Provides a user-friendly platform for creating professional designs quickly, from presentations to graphics."

Google Docs and Forms: "Enables easy document collaboration and data collection through cloud-based word processing and form tools, facilitating seamless sharing and editing."

ChatGPT: "Assists with generating text, answering questions, and providing information across various topics, streamlining communication and content creation." (The above quotes indicate descriptions generated using ChatGPT).

A quick disclosure: I used ChatGPT to rewrite the above descriptions based on the tools that save me the most time. It's a quick demonstration of how technology can help me save time on inconsequential tasks.

In addition, I sometimes use ChatGPT as a way to summarize notes that I take in meetings. Normally, I like to take notes with pen and paper. Afterwards, I will open a Google Doc and use the speech-to-text tool to record my notes. Then I paste those notes into ChatGPT with instructions to "Rewrite the following speech-to-text notes, maintaining the voice of the author, and correct any spelling, punctuation or grammar mistakes." A ten- to fifteen-minute task then becomes a three- to five-minute task.

Even though online tools change rapidly, you can adapt the use of tools like these and others to save time—or to create assistance for yourself—so that you free up time for other tasks that are more important to you.

Business To-Do's

Every school or organization has a system for how it conducts business. Learning these systems will save you time as well. At the school level, it will save you time and effort, for instance, to understand how to submit purchase orders if you want resources and supplies available.

Many teachers do not understand that districts budget for ongoing professional development. Asking to attend a conference, attend a workshop, or purchase helpful resources should not be seen as a barrier when you begin to understand the systems and budgets in place for these kinds of goods and services. Many districts allocate a specific amount of Title dollars for professional development.

As I have grown my own education services, I have also had to learn the importance of writing proposals, submitting service agreements, establishing a business entity through a Limited Liability Corporation with a tax-identification number, maintaining bookkeeping and invoicing, and hiring a financial planner with guidance on quarterly tax payments.

Although these kinds of business to-do's may seem far removed from the work of a typical educator, the more you understand how systems work, the more you can leverage those systems for the outcomes you want to see for your students, your staff, and your learning and growth.

Let's Wrap This Up

When I was in high school, my father and I spent a lot of time in the Kentucky Lake area diving for mussel shells. One day, a storm blew up on the lake while we were under water. When we emerged, we started the boat and headed toward land. The storm dropped with such fury, huge waves formed, and my dad had to wear a scuba mask in order to steer the boat. I felt like the biblical character Jonah, imagining being thrown over into the tall waves and wondering if I would ever resurface.

As we plowed ahead, the boat engine began to sputter. My dad looked back at me and said, "Grab the spare gas tank and change it out, or we're going to run out of gas." I ran to the back of the boat. I grabbed the spare gas tank, but I had never switched out a gas line before. As I stood staring at the dilemma, the boat motor stalled. My dad ran back to join me. He grabbed the gas tank and switched out the lines. After many sputtering starts, the boat motor revved to life, and we moved through the wind, waves, and rain into a cove, where we anchored the boat and sat on shore under some trees.

When the storm finally passed, my dad turned to me. "Why didn't you switch out the tanks like I asked?"

"I don't know how to switch out tanks. No one has ever shown me how."

"Oh," he said, looking puzzled.

I was the fourth child with three older brothers, and I explained to Dad that my big brothers had always done that chore when we boated together.

"What else do you not know how to do?" he asked.

And that question began a summer of to-do's, when I learned how to change the oil on our truck, how to change a flat tire, and how to jump-start a dead battery—as well as how to change out a gas tank on the boat. Among many other life lessons, my dad taught me that summer that it is better to have a system in advance than to assume you have one in the middle of an emergency.

Not all plans work out as scheduled. In school, emergencies, pandemics, and other difficulties inevitably throw us off course. At the same time, when we have created systems in advance, we are more likely to switch our focus back to our most important priorities after managing unscheduled events. Some people do this kind of planning naturally, while others struggle to make schedules work day to day.

- When is the last time you have mapped out your work or life priorities in advance?
- Have you included activities and contingency plans that reflect the entire year?
- What activities do you anticipate might be coming up in two or three years?

If you are mostly satisfied with the outcomes you are experiencing in work and life, my guess is that your calendar and planning already reflect how you are managing your time toward those goals and ends. However, if you are consistently frustrated with the outcomes you are experiencing, I invite you to examine your systems and take action on how you are implementing them toward your most important priorities.

Time for Reflection

1. What systems are you currently using that help you achieve the goals and outcomes you want?
2. What is an anticipated goal or outcome you want to achieve, and what systems or action steps can you take toward accomplishing it?

3. Who is someone with whom you could share your calendar? Are you willing for that person to follow-up with you to ask how you are doing with your most important priorities?
4. Set aside some time to work on your calendar. What can you schedule in advance that reflects the most important goals and priorities you are setting in life and work?
5. What contingency plans will you have in place if and when your plans are interrupted by unforeseen events?

CHAPTER 9

Cycles of Reflection for Lifelong Learning and Growth

I was probably in my fifteenth year as an educator when I attended a church dinner. While I stood with a plate in hand, looking over selections of cheese cut up into little cubes, a young man in his twenties was telling me about his new business. This young man and his wife had also just welcomed their second child to the family, and he was working on a master's degree while running his own company. As I took a bite of sharp cheddar, I congratulated him on the joyous season of their lives and began doing what a lot of older people do with younger ones: reminiscing about when I was his age.

"I remember when Missy and I were your age," I said. "We had paid off our college debts, and we were able to buy our first house the same year we had our first child. Doesn't it feel good when you can achieve some of the goals you've worked hard on?"

"Yes," he agreed. Then he had a curious look on his face. "What are the goals you have set for the next five or ten years of your life?" he asked.

I paused to consider the question. I looked back at my younger friend. "Honestly," I replied. "I'm just trying to survive right now. I haven't even thought about the next five to ten years."

We both laughed, but as I walked away, I was unsettled by the question. Honestly, I had worked hard for what I had achieved at the time. I had earned an advanced degree and had just been promoted to assistant principal. We had four young children. At this moment in time, I had reached those goals. But the truth is that I *was* in survival mode. Work, family, and life kept us busier and more committed than I had ever imagined. Yet I couldn't shake the question from my mind.

A few weeks later, our church hosted a men's retreat at a beautiful lake resort. This event was unlike any other I had attended. The weekend was arranged for us to gather on the first morning for scripture reading and a short talk from our pastor. Then he handed out a packet containing pages of questions with spaces for reflection.

The assignment required each person to find a quiet place for solitude, reflection, and prayer. The rest of the day's agenda was to reflect on questions and write responses:

- What milestones have you experienced this past year?
- What did you celebrate this past year?
- What were your most difficult challenges?
- What lessons did you learn along the way?
- How will you apply those lessons as you look forward?

Although the process involved more than these reflections, the purpose of the day was quiet, solitude, reflection, meditation, prayer, and planning. I was deeply moved by the process, as the dedicated time gave me pause to think about what goals and aspirations were important for the days and years ahead.

CYCLES OF REFLECTION

Cycles in Your Learning

We are trained as educators to embrace learning cycles for student learning. So, why not apply the same cycle to our own growth and pathways? If you haven't thought about the power of self-reflection lately, let me recommend a great book by Pete Hall and Alisa Simeral: *Teach, Reflect, Learn: Building Your Capacity for Success in the Classroom.*

A few years ago, I heard Pete Hall present lessons from the book, which included the Reflective Cycle (Hall & Simeral, 2015). He explained that our ability to grow is connected to our ability to honestly assess our strengths and weaknesses. Your ability to self-reflect involves a continuum of four stages:

1. Unaware Stage: The inability to see or lack of sensitivity to your practices—good or bad.

2. Conscious Stage: The recognition of your habits and progress—or lack of progress—and a realization of the implications.

3. Action Stage: Moving forward armed with new information, new action steps, new accountability, and a new commitment to trial and error for improvement.

4. Refinement Stage: Repeating what works, thinking ahead, collaborating with others, and planning with this new knowledge or practice in mind.

Pete shared a helpful video clip from a teacher on YouTube reflecting on his own teaching practice (#DeepThought Classroom Discussion, 2017). In that short spot, this young teacher went from describing what he believed was a most incredible teaching moment to acknowledging where he still had room to grow. He went from a "Wow, I'm awesome" moment to an "Uh-oh, I still have tons to learn" moment. It was a great example of how we can practice the reflective cycle even in times when we think our practice is profoundly effective.

Pete concluded: "Beware of the traveler who thinks he has arrived." In other words, we endanger effectiveness when we simply do what worked before without really analyzing our motivations or outcomes.

Reflection on Goal Setting

The practice of using reflection and learning cycles is common in educational settings, but have you considered how this could enhance your own goal setting? Throughout my educational journey, I've integrated these cycles into setting and achieving goals in several structured ways.

Daily Goals

I maintain a daily list of important tasks in my notes, usually derived from the priorities scheduled in my calendar. As I often emphasize, your calendar should mirror your values and priorities. If your calendar does not include activities that align with your skills and passions, it's likely you're not fully engaged in the work you love. List your daily goals, highlighting those tied to immediate deadlines or commitments. Also, make sure to include tasks that propel you toward your broader ambitions. Remember, it's OK not to tick off everything on your list each day; some tasks can be postponed or delegated if they don't align closely with your core values.

Weekly Goals

Beyond daily tasks, I compile a weekly list that captures the essence of a week's work. This includes major meetings or deadlines, which I note a week in advance to allow time for sending reminders and preparing necessary materials. This list aids in crafting more effective daily to-do lists and ensures a smoother workflow for the upcoming week.

Monthly Goals

At the beginning of each month, I create a "month at a glance" page that outlines major events in chronological order, including details like location, date, and the people or organizations involved. This overview assists in maintaining a balance between immediate tasks and long-term planning.

Yearly Goals

Each year during the winter break, I reflect on the past year and set goals for the coming one. These goals span various aspects of life, such as physical health, family, spiritual growth, friendships, finances, hobbies, and career, among others. For each area, I define specific, measurable, attainable, and time-bound actions. I keep these goals at the forefront of my current journal, using them as a continuous reference for growth and future planning throughout the year.

Life Score Assessment

Another tool that you may find helpful is a free online assessment I complete at the end of each calendar year called the Life Score, offered by Michael Hyatt's company (Full Focus, 2024).

The assessment takes about ten minutes to complete, and it offers you feedback on your practices involving your body, relationships, finances, spirituality, children, vocation, and hobbies. I use the assessment as a way to track my growth from year to year. It becomes a way for me to set yearly goals that are then reflected in my daily, weekly, and monthly to-do's.

An Example of My Yearly Goals

Sometimes examples help. If you saw the opening pages of my daily journal, you would see a list of my yearly goals:

Intellectual: learning more about world cultures
- Books for new knowledge:
  - The *Britannias* by Alice Albinia
  - The *Year of Living Danishly* by Helen Russell
  - The *Half-Known Life* by Pico Iyer
  - Behind *the Beautiful Forever* by Katherine Boo
- Books for pleasure or curiosity:
  - The *Lightning Thief* (Percy Jackson and the Olympians, Book 1) by Rick Riordan
  - Think *Remarkable* by Guy Kawasaki
  - "Letter from Birmingham Jail" by Martin Luther King, Jr.
  - *Testimony* by Jon Ward
  - *How to Stay Married* by Harrison Scott Key
  - *The 6 Types of Genius* by Patrick Lencioni

Physical: six-day workout schedules
- Monday, Wednesday, Friday: gym workouts for fitness and strength building
- Tuesday, Thursday, Saturday: running for 30–60 minutes
- Introduce swimming into routine
- Continue biking on warm days

Finance: salary/income goals, paying off debts, and emergency savings
- Target of x in coming school year for income related to Grow academies, Impact masterminds, executive coaching, book royalties, keynote presentations, and podcast sponsorships
- Scale offerings to include associates
- Increase giving and contributions by x

Spiritual: prayer and Bible-reading goals
- Use the Bible Project app for completing Sermon on the Mount series for the year
- Take Bible Project classes in Introduction to Hebrew Scriptures and Genesis 1

Parental: encourage adult children in their interests
- Connect weekly with each of our children
- Weekly lunches or dinners
- Encourage each one in their gifts and interests

Marital: spending more time doing what we love together
- Garden with Missy
- Plan more travel together

Avocational: committing time to improvements at home now that I work from home
- Schedule repairs and improvements
- Play music daily (guitar and piano)
- Research twenty good movies to watch with Missy

Miscellaneous: ongoing work/projects
- Finish writing my next book by x
- Launch a YouTube version of my podcast
- Create a new promo video for keynotes

This example only reflects one year in the cycle I am currently experiencing. By sharing these goals, I am not suggesting you do the exact same. Instead, I am trying to demonstrate one example of how the reflection cycle of learning has been useful in my work as an educator and person.

The cycles and goals I set as a teacher and administrator looked different from mine today, but without goals and reflection, you run the risk of letting what happens to you dictate what your next goals are—in other words, you move into survival mode instead of intentional growth mode.

WHOSE PERMISSION ARE YOU WAITING FOR?

How Does This Apply to Doing What You Love?

Being in survival mode is completely understandable and sometimes necessary—whether you're raising young children, caring for elderly parents, or managing educational responsibilities. These roles demand vast amounts of energy and time.

Yet, even amidst the daily struggle to survive, I recognized that merely getting through the day does not mean paying attention to the larger picture. Reflecting allows you to step back, consider your current situation, and think about your past experiences and future aspirations.

> Reflecting allows you to step back, consider your current situation, and think about your past experiences and future aspirations.

What's Ahead of You?

Imagine you're in a boat or raft, and you find yourself caught in a strong current. You need to be fully focused as you paddle and steer, trying to navigate through the rapids to safety. Now, imagine that you can see your situation from high above and notice that, in another half mile, you'll be approaching a waterfall.

If you were approaching an impending danger like a waterfall, I believe you would do everything to steer the boat out of the immediate danger or quickly make a plan to either pull ashore or find a way around it. Without perspective, simply surviving may soon turn into an unforeseen drowning.

With perspective, you are much more likely to navigate the present and the future with clarity. If you want to do the work you love, you must be willing to commit to the reflective cycles involved in learning. Just like a good classroom teacher assesses student learning through discovery, practice, application, and refinement, how are you engaging in cycles of learning in your journey?

What If Goal Setting Is Discouraging?

I want to add some context for anyone who feels discouraged, rather than encouraged, by goal setting. None of us has complete control of our circumstances. Despite what most self-help books tell us, we do not always have complete control of how we respond in every situation either.

When my mother was 53 years old, she was diagnosed with a brain tumor. This was the same year that I was graduating from college, had gotten engaged, and was seeking my first teaching position. My mother could not control her energy levels when debilitating migraines forced her to bed. Because of her condition, she was unable to attend my college graduation and could not be present for my wedding.

After brain surgery removed the tumor, she was blessed to have no cancerous cells to battle; however, the impairment to her vision and brain required her to relearn how to read and write as well as many other fine motor skills and cognitive functions. It was difficult seeing my mother struggling with simple tasks like remembering names or writing the alphabet. Sometimes the best I could do to help her in a difficult moment was to just sit quietly with her and let her know she was loved. At the same time, I was so proud of her for her commitment to rehabilitate and relearn.

Some of you reading this chapter have experienced trauma or helped others cope with their own trauma. Your ability to control what you can is a helpful commitment when you are working toward healthier habits, routines, reflection cycles, application, and growth. However, you must also give yourself a lot of grace for the circumstances outside of your control.

Like a recovering patient, you can rehabilitate or take action to improve, but no matter what stage of life you are in, other factors are always outside your control, including the miracle of perfect health. With a lot of work, prayer, and support, my mother regained a lot of what was lost from her brain surgery, but she also was not allowed to drive for the rest of her life and still struggled with her energy levels. She lived another thirty years, for which we are grateful. All this to say, please give yourself permission to dream, set goals, reflect, and take action within the context of what you can control. For those things outside of your control, it is helpful to remember that you are human, not a machine.

We still need others.

We are not God.

Do what is within your control, and when you're feeling overwhelmed, it is OK to sit quietly and remember you are loved, no matter what goals you achieve or don't achieve.

Time for Reflection

1. Can you set aside an hour, a half day, or a full day for reflection? Place that time on your calendar right now and make it a priority.
2. When you have time for reflection, consider the following questions, and write a response for each:
    + What milestones have you experienced this past year?
    + What did you celebrate this past year?
    + What were your most difficult challenges?
    + What lessons did you learn along the way?
    + How will you apply those lessons as you look forward?
3. Consider completing the LifeScore Assessment (https://assessments.fullfocus.co/lifescore/). Based on the assessment, what are specific, measurable, attainable, and time-based goals you can set for your areas of growth?

CYCLES OF REFLECTION

4. How do you create daily, weekly, monthly, and yearly goals based on your cycles of reflection?
5. What areas in your planning are within your control, and which ones are outside of your control? Who can you ask for help along the way?

CHAPTER 10

The Value of Coaching and Why You Need One

Several years ago, I came across a fantastic book titled *The Coaching Habit* by Michael Bungay Stanier (2016). A good friend of mine, Glen Abshere, who is the executive director of the Oklahoma Association of Elementary School Principals, introduced me to this book. We studied it together, and later we developed a presentation for school leaders on mentoring and coaching others.

During that workshop, we shared takeaways from Stanier's book. Since then, I have found the seven questions from his book to be one of the most useful tools when I'm mentoring leaders or when I need to reflect on decision making for myself. The value of coaching is that it allows someone to be on the other side of you, giving you the permission to hear your own thoughts and to think about what actions or steps you can take, what strategies you can employ, and what decisions you need to make. Stanier outlines seven questions (Stanier, 2016):

- The Kickstart Question: "What's on your mind?"
- The AWE Question: "And what else?"
- The Focus Question: "What's the real challenge here for you?"

- The Foundation Question: "What do you want?"
- The Lazy Question: "How can I help?"
- The Strategic Question: "If you're saying yes to this, what are you saying no to?"
- The Learning Question: "What was most useful for you?"

These questions have been instrumental in guiding both my reflections and my discussions with other leaders, providing a structured way to delve deeper into the challenges and opportunities we face.

Over the past few years, I have regularly met with leaders across the United States and overseas through Zoom meetings. Occasionally, I've had the opportunity to sit face to face with leaders, and I have memorized these questions because I've discovered that leaders often need permission to express what those questions probe. Let's discuss them one at a time for just a moment:

The Kickstart Question: "What's on your mind?" This question allows someone to simply voice the things that are most pressing or at the forefront of their thinking. Sometimes these are small things, like what's going on with their family or activities happening at their school. Sometimes they involve challenges they are facing at work or a current issue they are trying to resolve. So, the Kickstart Question is a great place to begin.

The AWE Question: "And what else?" This then allows the leader to consider what they really want to talk about. At this point, you're probably going to hear them touch on areas where they are trying to make a decision, whether they realize it or not. "And what else?" often gives you an opportunity to see what's truly on their mind.

The Focus Question: "What's the real challenge here for you?" This is an opportunity to help narrow the topic at hand. Usually, when someone shares the AWE Question with me, I will paraphrase or summarize back to that person what I hear them saying. For instance, a leader may say to me, "Our district is mandating a new initiative, and I've been asked to lead that initiative within my own school, but I don't understand or agree that this is the most important initiative for us at this time. How do I manage the difficulty between what I believe is best for my building and what the district is mandating?"

I will then summarize back to them, "What I hear you saying is . . ." and then proceed to clarify their thought, enabling them to articulate the real challenge they face.

For example, I might say, "What I hear you saying is that you feel a tension between what your district is asking you to do and what you believe is best for your students, schools, or teachers. Is that right?"

At this point, I'll follow up with a question: "What's the real challenge here for you?"

This opens up an opportunity for the leader to describe in their own words the dilemma they're facing. Perhaps it involves needing a conversation with someone in leadership above them, or maybe it's about reconciling what they can and cannot do in this situation. It could also involve discussing with their staff how to navigate the complexities of a directive that doesn't align with their current mission or goals, or it might be a deeper issue where they feel micromanaged, which hinders their ability to truly lead.

Whatever they express as the real challenge is usually the area where they feel the most pressure and see the need for some kind of action.

I usually follow this with the **Foundation Question**: "What do you want?" Sometimes I'll say, "If you could wave a magic wand, what would the outcome look like?" This allows the person to imagine the possibilities of what could happen in the situation, and visualizing these possible outcomes can help them envision a solution.

Pat Flynn, an entrepreneur and podcaster, likes to pose the question this way: "If it could be easy, what would it look like?" This approach helps frame the potential solution as something manageable, not necessarily the hardest task they've ever faced (Flynn, 2024).

Then comes the **Lazy Question:** "How can I help?" This question often catches people off guard, but it is effective. Usually, the people I coach say that just being able to talk about the issue and express their thoughts gives them the clarity and objectivity they need about what they are facing.

Sometimes, however, they ask for advice, inquiring, "What would you do in this situation?" or "Do you have any resources you could point me to?" or "Have you known someone who has gone through a similar situation?"

This is where coaching transitions from merely providing a space to also giving permission to offer guidance. Coaching isn't about giving advice directly; it's about creating a safe environment that allows for self-guided discovery, and, on occasion, providing advice when it's sought.

Usually at this point, if I'm able to offer some suggestions or ideas, I'll do so. Sometimes, I might simply say, "This is outside of my experience, but let's imagine what the possibilities might look like. What can you control, and what can you not control?"

Eventually, this conversation will lead to some sense of acceptance, influence, or choice in what the person decides to do next. This is when the **Strategic Question** comes into play, and it's usually the question that stumps every leader I talk to. I'll say, "Based on what you've told me, it seems like you feel you need to take the following action." Then I'll repeat back to them the action they've just described to me, and I'll ask, "If you're saying yes to taking this action, what are you saying no to?"

Almost every time I ask that question, the leader will pause and say, "I don't know the answer to that question," or "I'm not sure what I can say no to."

I don't supply the answer for them. Instead, what I want them to think about is the fact that, when you're setting boundaries in the work that you do, when you're choosing an action to take, when you are stepping into a conversation that needs to happen, every time you say yes to whatever that next thing is, you're saying no to something else—and that's okay. In order for you to say yes to a situation, inevitably you're saying no to something else.

Let me give you an example: Sometimes I talk to leaders who feel like they have no time left in their day to do the things they want to do the most, such as development with teachers. When this happens, I ask them if there is anything on their to-do list that someone else could be trained to handle or if they could develop someone else to help alleviate some of their responsibilities.

Many times, the leader will tell me that it takes longer to train someone else than to just do it themselves. At that point, I want them to recognize that they're saying no to training someone else and saying yes to continuing to do it themselves, which also means they're saying no to the things they really want to do.

Sometimes, in the short term, you must invest time to develop someone else and train them to do the hard things so that later you will have time to do the things you want to do. It's an exchange, and leaders who refuse to develop or delegate responsibilities will never get around to doing the things that they want to do.

At the same time, I've worked with leaders who are wonderful at delegation and distributive leadership, and yet they still feel like crises, emergencies, or mandates are pulling them off track from the things they really want to do. At this point, I have to ask whether they would consider one of three options:

1. Acceptance: This is just the reality in which you work and live. "Can I accept I may not be able to change a person or outcome?"
2. Influence: "What can I change?" Are there systems in place involving students, teachers, or your community that are contributing to the ongoing crisis or mandates that could be

influenced by you to go in a different direction to improve?
3. Choice: "Should I dig in or move on?" Sometimes, these hard conversations motivate others to make a choice. If their environment is one where they feel trusted and supported, they are willing to keep working on solutions. If they are in a place that is an untrusting or a toxic environment they are unable to change, they may decide it is time for another setting.

Author Jen Schwanke calls this the choice between two questions: "Can I continue to bloom where I am planted, or do I go where I am wanted?"

For example, I was talking to a leader recently who realized that many of the mandates coming from district leadership were happening because the leaders were not aware of how busy building principals were as they were wrapping up a school year. This was not the time to be asking them to implement new initiatives. This leader realized that she would need to have a conversation with district leaders to explain this dilemma; otherwise, they would continue to move forward with initiatives that were competing with the already full calendars that teachers and principals were managing in the last months of school.

In the case of this leader, she had to say yes to a hard conversation but at the same time be willing to say no to a few things on her to-do list in order to have that conversation, realizing that the potential outcome could open up more opportunities for her to do the things that she wanted to do. I'm not dictating what choice should be made; I'm simply saying these are the options you have when faced with strategic questions. You can either accept, influence, or choose.

The last question that Michael Bungay Stanier poses in his book is the **Learning Question**: "What was most useful for you?" I have found this to be a helpful way for me to understand the impact of our conversation as we wrap it up. Many times, leaders tell me that what was most helpful was simply having the opportunity to express their thoughts and to think clearly and objectively with someone else supporting them. This is why I believe coaching is so important and why I think everyone should be open to being coached.

My Early Mentors

As a student teacher, I was coached by Mrs. Myrna Morton, a seasoned thirty-year veteran English teacher at Jenks High School in Oklahoma. She taught me how to grade papers, organize classrooms, and ask deeper questions.

When I was a young teacher, my first coach was a fellow Broken Arrow teacher, Darren Pettitt, who taught drama, speech, and debate at our school. We had lunch together every day, and during these sessions, he would ask me about the challenges I was facing with my students. From his own experience, he helped me find better ways to manage classroom behavior, set learning standards, accomplish tasks, and consider the long-term challenges we face in education.

As an assistant principal, my coaches involved fellow administrators and colleagues like Lydia Wilson from Bixby Public Schools or Donna Brogan from Skiatook High School. They gave me real-life solutions and modeled problem solving for me. Then they released me to take action on my own.

When I decided to launch my own consulting business, I reached out to a friend who had been in this field long before I had—Daniel Bauer (2022b), the host of the *Better Leaders Better Schools* podcast. Danny has authored several books, led masterminds, and coached other leaders for many years. I told him I wanted to put my money where my mouth is and asked him to coach me during my first year of consultation and full-time work with *Principal Matters*.

Having someone on the other side allows me to engage in the same reflective practices I facilitate for others, such as reflecting, thinking out loud, dreaming, probing, asking questions, seeking advice, and understanding new tools or strategies that I might not have known before.

Coaches come in all different shapes and sizes, each bringing their unique perspectives and experiences that can profoundly impact their mentees. For some people, including me, clarity is found through journaling, prayer, or therapy. Each of these methods is valuable, but I argue that you also professionally benefit from the focus that comes with having a coach.

What do high-performing athletes and executives have in common? They have coaches. Coaches see something in the athlete or performer that the individual may not see in themselves.

As educators, we often work in isolation. Teachers may have a classroom full of students, but they often lack direct feedback on their performance from peers or coaches. School administrators manage meetings that often involve highly confidential information with students, teachers, or families. To whom do they turn when they need advice, counsel, or coaching on the next steps?

Let's Wrap This Up

Let me be clear about what I am *not* saying. Coaching should not replace licensed, credentialed experts like physicians, attorneys, clergy, or therapists when you are facing health, legal, or complex situations that require specialized input. However, coaching can be incredibly helpful for guiding decision making, reflection cycles, and problem solving in your professional life.

One day my friend and colleague Glen Abshere, executive director of the Oklahoma Association of Elementary School Principals, and I were facilitating training on coaching. We asked attendees to sit in triads and share. Each person was assigned roles: coach, coachee, and observer. Each person rotated roles, practicing many of the questions

THE VALUE OF COACHING AND WHY YOU NEED ONE

discussed in this chapter. When we divided the participants into groups, two people needed an additional person to make a triad. I volunteered to join their group.

Even though I was helping facilitate the training, it was insightful and fun to be a participant. We set a timer, and the person assigned as coachee shared their most current challenge. The person assigned as coach asked clarifying questions and provided feedback. The observer took notes and then summarized and added additional feedback.

Each group of three rotated these roles in timed sessions. When it was my turn to be the coachee, I realized I was on the spot. Each of the leaders in my group had shared current issues and had been vulnerable with their challenges, obstacles, and concerns. I decided I would need to do the same.

At the time, I was struggling with the dilemma of what to do next in my professional journey. I loved my current work as an executive director for our state principal association, but I also loved writing books, consulting, and coaching educators when invited to other organizations and states. I described the dilemma I was facing, trying to decide if and when I should transition into full-time consulting or whether it should remain a part-time commitment for me.

One of the leaders in my triad was asking me reflective questions, when she paused, and asked, "If fear and money were not concerns for you, where do you believe you would have the most impact in the choices before you?"

I was stumped, not because I did not know the answer, but because the answer was so obvious to me, and I had never seen it before. "I would have to say, I could make a greater impact for more leaders and more schools through full-time consulting work."

It was the first time I had been confronted with the question, and the clarity that moment brought me was helpful in the steps I took over the next few months to officially transition my work into what I'm doing today.

WHOSE PERMISSION ARE YOU WAITING FOR?

If you had asked me the same question thirty years ago, when I was a classroom teacher, the answer would have been that the greatest impact I could make at the time was influencing the lives of the students in my care. At my current stage of life, the answer to that question is different but makes sense for what I feel qualified and called to do.

Sometimes we do not know our own thoughts until someone is on the other side of us to help us hear them. The power of coaching not only provides you with tools to help others, but the same tools can be used in your own development.

> Sometimes we do not know our own thoughts until someone is on the other side of us to help us hear them.

There have been times when I simply write out responses to the seven questions from Michael Stanier's Coaching Habits. It is not as effective as when someone else is on the other side of me, reflecting out loud and asking clarifying questions. At the same time, the process of answering those questions can prod you forward into helpful next steps.

Time for Reflection

1. When was the last time someone was able to project your own thoughts back to you?
2. Name the people who have coached or mentored you in your own educational journey.
3. How are you intentionally inviting ongoing input into the work you are doing, the goals you are setting, or the decisions you are making?
4. Take time and write out responses to the seven questions from the *Coaching Habit*.

CHAPTER 11

The Value of Masterminds for Collective Growth

Recently, I heard an illustration during a Sunday morning sermon from one of our ministers, Pastor Mark Kuiper, who loves watching the Tour de France. He explained that when bikers ride in a pack, the force carrying them is so strong that a biker in the middle could stop pedaling and still be pulled along by the others. In cycling, this is called the "peloton."

The term *peloton* has gained popularity since the biking machine by the same name became very popular during the pandemic. It allows people to ride at home alone while joining a virtual group of riders through a video connection, emulating a communal experience. However, no virtual experience can match the physical effect of an actual peloton in action. This analogy is useful when considering the power of the peloton versus the power of the individual.

As Mark pointed out in his story, one of the most frustrating parts of watching a race is when one rider pulls ahead, sometimes leading for sixty or even eighty miles, only to be overtaken at the end by the peloton, with someone else using their reserved strength to beat the solo rider.

WHOSE PERMISSION ARE YOU WAITING FOR?

This makes me think about our work in education. How often do we rely on our own strength as individuals, and how much do we depend on the power that comes from collaboration, community, and the collective efforts of others?

In my career in education, I have always gained more traction and momentum by collaborating with others. As a young teacher, this began in my department team, where veteran English teachers would gather weekly to discuss objectives and learning standards. We encouraged each other to bring student samples to these conversations, share ideas, discuss best practices, and support each other in our teaching and student learning.

As a young administrator, I benefited from being part of an admin team as well as from interactions with veteran teachers or counselors with whom I could rally to discuss ideas or brainstorm possible solutions to problems we were facing. Being part of professional learning communities also provides opportunities for educators to connect regularly about student learning and their own teaching ideas.

In my personal life, the peloton effect has been evident in my ability to reach out to other men in my community and trust them enough to ask questions about how they manage difficulties in parenting, navigate challenges within their marriages, handle financial stress, or find answers during career and pathway changes.

In 2020, I decided to reach out to the podcast community and invite any education leaders preparing to return to school after the initial pandemic closures. I asked if they would be willing to collaborate through ongoing mastermind meetings, sharing ideas that were working for them as they reopened their schools while maintaining protocols suggested by their districts, states, or the Centers for Disease Control and Prevention (CDC). More than two dozen people responded to my invitation, and we began weekly Zoom meetings that lasted for six weeks. During these meetings, we logged in, talked, and shared ideas.

At the end of those six weeks, I issued an invitation to anyone who would like to continue meeting, not necessarily weekly, but for paid access, which would allow us to focus on specific content, self-reflection, assessments, and ongoing problem solving with a stronger commitment. Six leaders responded to this invitation, and I began my very first experience leading a mastermind.

Fast forward to today, and I have been leading ongoing groups in mastermind settings with district and state leadership teams in schools. Together, the input of the group becomes the power that helps us solve problems. One of my favorite sayings when leading the mastermind is to remind them that the smartest person in the room is the room itself.

So, what are some of the components of a mastermind that might help you when you are collaborating with others to discover answers to questions, solutions to problems, and potential pathways as you think about doing what you love? Here are some components that we've used in the masterminds I facilitate, which might be helpful for you:

Ongoing Content Discussions

In each mastermind that I lead, we pick a book or a piece of content to read in advance of our discussions. Over the years, we have chosen several books, including titles like *David and Goliath* by Malcolm Gladwell, *Transforming School Culture* by Dr. Anthony Muhammad, *Extreme Ownership* by Jocko Willink and Leif Babin, *Messaging Matters* by William D. Parker, and *The Five Voices* by Jeremy Kubicek and Steve Cockram, to name a few. For whatever content you are discussing, I suggest reading in advance and creating four or five questions to place on an agenda. These questions can be discussed at the beginning of the meeting, just after some short celebrations that each person brings to the meeting.

Self-Assessments

Each time we meet, I share four statements and ask each person within the group to rank themselves on a scale from one to five, where one indicates "no or little time" and five means "lots of time committed" to the following:

- I have been visible with every teacher and every student and the people I value in my community this past week.
- I have been reading, listening to, meditating on, or reflecting on helpful books or lessons.
- I have been making healthy choices in my sleep, nutrition, rest, and exercise.
- I have been faithful to my loved ones with my time and attention.

Hot-Seat Discussions

Finally, we take time for what I call *hot-seat* discussions. In these discussions, whether within the main group or in breakout rooms if we're meeting virtually, leaders are given permission to listen to one person in the group who brings up a situation they are struggling with and is looking for feedback. These hot-seat discussions are helpful in several ways:

- They provide an opportunity for the leader in question to express concerns and thoughts that they may not have been able to share with anyone else.
- They allow the listeners to ask clarifying questions.

These questions might include responses from others like, "What I hear you saying is," or opportunities to ask about the potential impacts of the situation on teachers, students, or others.

They might inquire, "What would be the observable impact if you did the following?" or "What would you do if you believed you were doing what's best for all involved?" Questions like these open up ideas for the person sharing their concerns so they can begin forming possible solutions.

We conclude these discussions by having the person in the hot seat share what was most useful for them. Typically, the topics can range from student discipline to parent interactions, problems with colleagues, or concerns over board members.

The list goes on, but the power does not necessarily lie with having an answer for the person in the hot seat. Instead, the power is in the peloton—the collective motion and action of everyone in the group, rooting for, encouraging, and probing with the leader until they find some ideas that help them take their next steps.

The Benefits of the Peloton Effect

The power of collaboration became even more apparent during the COVID-19 pandemic, when the shared knowledge of scientists and researchers across the world created a quickly formulated vaccine that has saved thousands, if not millions, of lives.

The idea of the mastermind has become very popular in both professional and education settings. Some people pull together in masterminds for ideas around entrepreneurship and business, while others gather in professions like health and medicine.

The Oklahoma State University's Project Echo has an ongoing group of physicians who meet across the state to confer with each other regularly through virtual meetings. This has been especially helpful for rural physicians who find themselves in need of ideas and best practices that may not be as available to them as those colleagues who live in urban or suburban settings. Project Echo has now replicated versions of these programs available for educators across the state (Oklahoma State University, 2024).

Earlier in the book, I mentioned my friend Dr. Nick Davies from Washington State–Vancouver. Nick decided to reach out to assistant principals from his state to meet with him regularly for the same kind of conversations I just described. Nick discovered that they could solve problems and identify solutions much faster than he had considered before.

The mastermind model has also been a helpful model for me to use in my one-on-one coaching. Although this is just the power of two, it does provide for a coachee to be on the other side of someone who's also walking through important questions and clarifications with them. As you think about your own journey ahead, consider who you could meet with regularly for collaboration, discussion, and discovering potential solutions.

My friend Daniel Bauer has written an entire book on masterminds (Bauer, 2022a), which you can check out. For the sake of our discussion here, I want you to consider how being part of a community of other educators could create a peloton effect in your own pathways forward.

Intentional Accountability

Being part of a mastermind provides intentional accountability. Meeting regularly with other like-minded educators and leaders—if you value that activity—requires you to schedule time for it. Activities that you value, and for which you set aside time, effort, and concentration, are typically areas where you will see more growth. Consider how this works in personal fitness: When you have an intention to exercise regularly but do not place it on your schedule or connect it to accountability with someone else, it's very likely that it won't happen.

However, when you put personal fitness as an expectation that's reflected in your calendar and actions and sometimes involves feedback or activity with others, you may be more likely to show up, even when you don't feel like it. I have a good friend, Dr. Scott Beck, who has been a long-distance runner for many years. He begins every day by meeting up with his friend Pete, and the two of them run for miles, collaborating, talking, coaching, consoling, and laughing together. Theirs is, in some ways, a running mastermind.

You're Not Alone

A mastermind provides an opportunity to remember you're not alone. So often in the world of education, we find ourselves serving students or supporting other teachers. In the process, we feel like the conflicts that we're managing are something that no one else experiences. Instead, when we share those concerns with other educators, we discover that we have a lot more in common than we realize.

My wife once referred me to a book, *Friendships Don't Just Happen! The Guide to Creating a Meaningful Circle of Girl Friends* by Shantel Nelson. In the book, Nelson refers to a study released on friendship called the "Social Support and the Perception of Geographical Slant" (Schnall et al., 2008).

Participants in the study were asked to estimate the incline of a hill in front of them. Over and over again, those who were accompanied by a friend (or even thought of a friend) estimated the hill to be less steep than participants who were alone. The researchers concluded that "an interpersonal phenomenon, social support, can influence visual perception" (Schnall et al., 2008). It may seem like common sense that the support or presence of a friend encourages or positively motivates you. But this study suggests that the presence of a friend (or even their imagined presence) actually changes your physical and emotional perceptions.

Shared Solutions

Finally, a mastermind gives you the opportunity for shared solutions. When you think about the combined experience that three, four, or six people can bring to one room, you begin to understand the power of shared ideas versus the ideas of an individual.

Even with thirty years of education experience, I cannot solve the deep kinds of problems that I face alone, compared to when I have the input of 120 to 200 combined years of experience in one room. Think about what that means for you.

Let's Wrap This Up

I recently met with a mastermind of leaders with whom I have now met for almost four years. These leaders are superintendents or principals from schools across the same state, serving in similar demographics and with similar school funding models. One of these leaders in particular wanted to share a hot-seat issue she was struggling with. Specifically, she did not know how to encourage input from her team without getting so distracted by their needs and concerns that she was unable to work on other strategic planning ideas or responsibilities unique to her own position.

The other members within the group began to ask her clarifying questions, trying to understand exactly what the underlying problem was and the challenge she was facing. Eventually, she realized that she needed to set boundaries in her conversations with others to show that she valued their input but also valued the other responsibilities and events on her own calendar.

As a result, she came up with the idea of beginning upcoming meetings or conversations with others by saying, "Just so you know, I have another commitment coming up in a few minutes."

THE VALUE OF MASTERMINDS FOR COLLECTIVE GROWTH

This leader reached out to me by text message and said this one simple practice has added an additional two hours to each of her working days. This is just one example of a leader who has faced the same challenge over and over again but, through collective feedback, was able to identify the area where she needed some strategic wisdom and change.

Not all masterminds create these kinds of results for leaders, but without intentional connection with others, without remembering that you are not alone, or without benefiting from shared ideas, you may be left feeling like that lone cyclist in the race of working life. Instead, learn to recognize the peloton effect of pedaling with others and draw advantage from it.

Time for Reflection

1. Identify some people you could connect with on a regular basis and ask them questions relating to issues you might be struggling with.
2. How might relying on the feedback of wise counselors through good books, podcasts, or online lessons contribute to the shared knowledge of that group?
3. How might assessing your own practices with one another on a regular basis hold you more accountable?
4. In what ways might clarifying, asking hard questions, and opening yourself up for feedback from others provide you useful solutions?
5. Want to join a mastermind with me or other educators? Reach out at will@williamdparker.com to learn more.

CHAPTER 12

Liturgies of Life That Shape Your Present and Future

I've been enjoying a book by Alice Albinia titled *The Britannias*. It's a study of the histories of the islands surrounding Britain, an obscure read that I have enjoyed because so much of it is information way outside my knowledge base. The author covers topics ranging from Neolithic history and the histories of Celts and Druids to the formation of languages (many no longer spoken) across the British Isles.

While living in Orkney for fourteen months, Alice Albinia visited a ceremonial area called Maeshowe—an underground chamber built around 5,000 BCE. The people who built chambers like Maeshowe and others discovered during ancient times likely used these places for religious worship or ceremonies (Albinia, 2024).

In Maeshowe, she was fortunate enough to visit during the winter solstice. During her fourth day, when the clouds cleared, she witnessed a shaft of light shooting through the small opening of the stone doorway, flooding the chamber with sunlight. The moment was awe-inspiring as architectural designs like this suggest that Neolithic peoples had advanced understandings of mathematics. Imagine the engineering feat of constructing a monument so precisely that, at one specific time each year, light shines through a small opening and fills an entire chamber.

Rituals are not new to human history. For as far back as historians and archaeologists have been able to trace human existence, people have practiced rituals and rites. Even those who claim they don't follow rituals or rites are likely unaware of the habits, routines, and practices they engage daily, weekly, or seasonally that shape who they are and who they will become. Think about your own life for a moment:

- How do you get out of bed each morning?
- Consider the small routines you have for coffee or breakfast, or even brushing your teeth.
- When do you prefer to leave for work?
- What about the choices you make in clothing, news, information, inspiration, or music?
- How have you chosen your habits, celebrations, and the events you attend—birthdays, yearly holidays?

Some of these choices have historical and religious connotations, while others are the product of your preferences. In some ways, however, these elements are part of a cultural ocean in which you swim. How aware are you of how each of these choices, moments, and events shape you?

No matter what time period, culture, or country, people are participating in a kind of liturgy every day: their daily actions, experiences, shows they watch, food they eat, people they spend the most time with, books they read—all of these shape people in the ways they think, feel, and behave. Those behaviors are your habits, and those habits over time create many of your outcomes.

A Shell of Myself

In 2020, I wrote a book titled *Pause. Breathe. Flourish: Living Your Best Life as an Educator*. In it, I discussed my experiences as an educator and how I nearly burned out after becoming a school administrator.

In my second year as an assistant principal, while raising four young children with my wife, I was still adjusting to the demanding roles of school leadership. I spent many hours covering events at night. I would wake up hours before my children to prepare for the day, arriving at school before anyone else to handle my administrative tasks and oversee the school operations.

One night, after the children had gone to bed, my wife told me, "Will, you have become a shell of the man you used to be. The children and I have accepted that you are a husband and a dad on the weekends only. The rest of the time, the school owns you." She did not say this with bitterness but with simple resignation.

That night, I didn't work as usual. Instead, I wrote a letter of resignation, explaining to my administration and board that I couldn't fulfill my duties to the school, students, and community without neglecting my responsibilities as a father, husband, and individual. I took this letter to school, placed it on my desk, and made a commitment: I would either rediscover ways to better care for myself and my family, or I would resign and find a new profession.

Thankfully, over the following years, I reconnected with habits and practices beneficial for myself, my family, and my school. I share this story in my book *Pause. Breathe. Flourish* to illustrate the importance of self-care, family, and professional balance. The book breaks down ten areas vital for a fulfilling life: your body, mind, influence, time, friendships, resources, future, intimacies, spirituality, and legacy.

As you embrace your journey of doing what you love, I want to caution you to not lose yourself in the process. The following are some of the lessons I've learned through the mistakes I've made, the practices that have helped me, and the habits (or rituals) I've observed in other educators who have managed to thrive despite the high demands.

Your Mindset

How you think about yourself and others significantly influences the decisions you make. Sadly, we often struggle to see the best in ourselves and in others. What if, instead, we became curious to understand ourselves and others before passing judgment? We all deserve dignity and respect, and we should extend the same grace to others that we hope to receive.

This doesn't mean abandoning high standards for yourself and others. It does mean, however, that you need to move forward with a people-centered approach that is kind to yourself as well as those around you.

> As you embrace your journey of doing what you love, I want to caution you to not lose yourself in the process.

Your Nutrition

I'm not a nutrition expert, but I have learned firsthand how significantly what I eat affects how I feel. During my burnout years in education, I often skipped meals or grabbed the most convenient options, like pizza from the school lunch line. My doctor also informed me of my high cholesterol, prompting me to change my dietary habits.

Over time, I've made a stronger commitment to mindful eating because I understand its impact not just on my present but also on my future. In discussions around my book, *Pause. Breathe. Flourish*, I've asked many educators how they manage their nutrition.

Some plan their menus for the entire week; others pack their lunches the night before to ensure they have healthy options during the day. Some eat communally to share food and hold each other accountable for making healthy choices. Others practice moderation with sugar and caffeine intake.

I don't need to quote science or health studies to remind you that a diet rich in vegetables and fruits is healthier than one filled with processed foods like potato chips and carbonated beverages. If you find yourself lacking energy, consider the quality of fuel you're putting into your body. High-quality foods—fruits, vegetables, and proteins from natural, not processed, sources—will likely lead to better health outcomes.

Your Sleep

A lot of research has been conducted on how a lack of sleep may contribute to early-onset dementia or Alzheimer's (National Institutes of Health, 2018). Even without these findings, we all recognize how challenging it is to stay focused and present when we're tired. If you're someone who struggles with sleep, analyzing your sleep routines could be beneficial. It's also possible that the ruminations or anxieties you bring to bed each night might make it difficult to sleep well. Some people find relief through exercise, meditation, and medications that can help them achieve better sleep patterns.

Consider setting a specific time to go to bed each night—even if you have to manage late school activities—and turning off your phone thirty minutes to an hour before sleep. Implement an evening unwinding ritual, like changing into something comfortable, washing your face, brushing your teeth, reading in bed, and avoiding screens. Listen to quiet music, use curtains that block out light, or employ soothing white noise machines like fans or apps on your phone.

The benefits of sleeping well include more energy, improved concentration, emotional presence with others, and the ability to handle the typically energy-draining afternoon slump—which, according to

Daniel Pink (2019) in his book *When: The Scientific Secrets of Perfect Timing*, is often the worst time for decision making. Be aware of how lack of sleep can impact your ability to make sound decisions.

If you're an overworked educator, a young parent, or caring for an aging parent, and you find yourself sleep-deprived, give yourself lots of grace. Practice these routines as best as you can, knowing that there will eventually be more time for improved sleep.

Your Environment

I attended a student science fair a few months ago where high school students showed me their research on how sound and music could affect the growth of plants. They compared the effects of gospel music, country music, and rock and roll. Not surprisingly, the plants exposed to gospel and country music grew at a stronger pace than those exposed to rock and roll. When I asked the students why they thought this was, they suggested that something in the sound waves affects plant growth. If plants can be affected by something as simple as music, imagine how our minds are influenced by the sights, smells, sounds, and lighting we encounter each day.

The place where you live and work can significantly influence how you feel. Consider how different your emotions are when you step out into a pleasant day with an open sky and sunshine versus when you spend time in a windowless room with fluorescent lighting overhead. Unfortunately, the latter often describes many of the classrooms I've visited and some in which I have worked.

Our environments not only affect how we think but also how we feel. Sometimes, these environments can be transformed through your influence. I've seen teachers who have turned windowless classrooms with harsh fluorescent lights into beautiful, inviting spaces with colorful walls, strategically placed lamps, or hanging bulbs strung across the room to create a warm atmosphere for students. Some simple questions to ask yourself about your environment include the following:

- Is this place organized, uncluttered, and welcoming?
- What kind of lighting am I exposed to here?
- How often do I have access to natural light or the opportunity to step outside and enjoy nature?
- How often are my students able to experience sunlight and nature?
- Do I sometimes use music to create a more contemplative atmosphere or to enhance my mood?
- Is the place fresh, and does it smell good?

Your Movement

A few years ago, a friend of mine, Kim Coody—who was the principal of Glenpool High School outside of Tulsa, Oklahoma, and now serves as the assistant superintendent for the same district—shared a story about an experiment she conducted. She decided to shadow a student for the day, a practice she continued for two years. During these shadowing experiences, she followed a student's schedule, sitting in the same classes, participating in assignments, and eating lunch where the students did. Among the many insights she gained from seeing her school through the eyes of a student, the one that stood out to her the most was how challenging it was to sit in student desks all day.

As adults, especially educators who can stand, walk, and teach while moving, we sometimes forget how confining and uncomfortable it can be for students who are seated for long periods. How can we encourage more movement for our students? Similarly, we should ask, What kind of movement keeps us engaged and helps maintain our mental alertness?

WHOSE PERMISSION ARE YOU WAITING FOR?

In 2023, the National Public Radio's TED Radio Hour hosted a series called "Body Electric," where researchers invited listeners to participate in a movement exercise. Over 30,000 people signed up, although only half completed the challenge, which involved standing up and walking around every thirty minutes or so during their workday. Those who maintained their commitment for thirty days reported significant improvements in their mental and physical well-being (Zomorodi, 2023).

Your Relationships

In the book *Think Remarkable: 9 Paths to Transform Your Life and Make a Difference* by Guy Kawasaki and Madison Nuismere (2024), Kawasaki references research by Daniel Pink, who conducted the World Regret Project. In this project, 19,000 people from 105 countries shared their greatest regrets in life. One significant type of regret highlighted was what participants termed *connection regret*—regrets involving relationships that should have existed or those that drifted apart (Pink, 2022).

At the end of our lives, few people regret the unfinished items on their to-do lists—things like unanswered emails, grocery shopping, or house cleaning. Instead, the list of regrets is the loss of connections. Most participants explained that these losses didn't occur through dramatic breakups but through simply drifting away from meaningful relationships, neglecting them until they faded into nonexistence.

How are you intentionally staying connected to the people you love the most? As I mentioned in Chapter 9, I encourage education leaders to reflect daily on several key areas:

+ How am I staying connected to every student and every teacher every day?

- How am I engaging with helpful books or lessons through meditation, listening, or reading?
- How am I taking care of my nutrition, exercise, rest, and overall health?
- Am I taking time to invest in the relationships that matter most to me?

I pose these questions regularly because, despite their importance, maintaining connections with loved ones often falls to the bottom of our priority list in the rush of a busy day. Yet, your partner, spouse, children, family members, and best friends deserve to know they are in your thoughts and that you care about them.

So, pause right now from reading this book, send a quick text to someone you love, and then schedule something on your calendar to connect with them soon—a meal, a conversation, or even just a cup of coffee.

Let's Wrap This Up

Even in the most ancient cultures, most world religions set aside at least one day a week to take a break from normal activities for rest, reflection, worship, and service. These practices recognize a need that humans have identified for thousands of years: the importance of rest to maintain their capacity to continue doing hard work.

Early in my education career, I realized I was working almost nonstop. My weekends seemed just as busy as my weekdays, filled with grading papers, lesson planning, or other school-related activities. When I decided to wrap up all my loose ends by Saturday so that I could dedicate Sunday to rest, worship, and reflection, I found that I actually had more energy on Monday mornings than I did before adopting this practice.

Whatever rest means to you—through your practices, rituals, and habits—give yourself permission to practice what many people and societies have recognized for ages: rest is a universal right.

Seven years after I wrote my letter of resignation, I was honored as Oklahoma's State Assistant Principal of the Year. At the award ceremony in Washington, D.C., I looked at my family—Missy in an evening gown, the children in their Sunday best, and me in a tuxedo—and realized that if it wasn't for that difficult conversation with my wife, I might have left the profession.

Wherever you live and in whatever time period you find yourself, you are engaged in practicing rituals and rites. Over time, the liturgies of life shape our personality, character, and relationships. If you really want to embrace doing what you love, do not wait for "someday" in the future. Start engaging now in practices that will positively shape your mindset, habits, nutrition, sleep, environment, movement, and relationships—contributing to the kind of life you wish to lead.

Give yourself permission now to flourish instead of waiting for the perfect time in the future.

Time for Reflection

1. Make a list of the morning rituals you currently have and what you would like to change.
2. What are you committed to that encourages good nutrition, exercise, and rest?
3. As soon as you step into your work environment each day, what are your routines and rituals?
4. How does your calendar reflect what you prioritize?
5. How do you give yourself permission to leave work and take time for your own needs and those of the people you care about?
6. How do you create action plans that allow you to be intentional and prepared for the next day?

CHAPTER 13

Finding Your Greatest Joy Is Not What You May Think

Once, when I was in college, I traveled to Guatemala and visited a remote mountain village area. One night, my college friends and I stood beneath the expanse of a starlit sky—the first time in my life that I had seen the beauty of the night sky with almost no light pollution.

The existence of that canopy of stars, with the rich Milky Way so visible, made me realize how small I am. At the same time, I felt comforted by the idea that God was smiling on me in the expanse of the cosmos. In the history of humankind before me and for ages to come, people have been mesmerized by a beauty that compels them to think about the deeper questions of life.

"Who am I?" is a question that I have pondered many times throughout my youth and life. This is partly because I grew up in a family with a rich religious tradition, and being exposed to big questions about God, humanity, and eternity caused me to ponder transcendent questions.

Having spent many years of my young life in the country, sometimes those thoughts came to me within the context of my setting—when standing below the expanse of a stunning sunset, looking across the stretches of open fields, walking through the shadows of forests, or exploring the edges of rambling creeks.

Often, when I'm working with leaders and educators, they ask, "What is the most important choice for me to make?" I believe your most important choices are impossible to separate from your personal beliefs and values.

When you think about who you are, my guess is that you desire to be the best version of yourself. But how can the best version of yourself be evident in the most important choices that you make?

Over the years, I've wrestled a lot with decisions about what is next, especially within my career. Because it is important to me to feel that what I'm doing has meaning, I want to know that my choices in work are deeper than just earning a paycheck. Most educators I know see their work as a calling. Their connection with people, their service to their communities, and their ability to help a student understand something they may have never understood before is a privilege and a high calling.

So, it makes sense that we care deeply about our decisions. When we say yes to a new position, explore the possibility of a transition, or are sometimes forced into a new role, we want to know:

- Is this the right fit for me?
- Does this match the best version of me?
- Is what I'm doing a good match for who I am?

Doing What You Love

When I was invited to leave my position as a principal to join the team with my state principals association, it meant I would be leaving a school community in order to support the work of school communities across my state. This was a difficult and painful decision because I loved my school, the team I was able to build, the teachers and staff, and the fact that my two daughters attended my school. I had been at my school long enough to hire and develop at least three-quarters of the employees under my care. I reveled in the adrenaline rush of conflict resolution and problem solving, the laughter, and sometimes the tears involved in the work.

When I announced to my family that I was making this transition, my oldest daughter cried—not because she was sad but because, as she explained to me, she knew how much I loved my school. Experiences in making hard choices connected to my values have taught me valuable lessons:

1. *In best-case scenarios, you should leave what you love in order to do something that you may love more.*

   Any transition in your work—whether it's a promotion or changing schools—is an opportunity to reflect on whether you've invested your heart in your work, even if you're leaving a difficult and toxic environment and you're happy to say goodbye. You probably poured your heart into the work and made a difference in the lives of others. Hopefully you saw that previous opportunity as a precious gift and allowed yourself to improve as a person.

   This is the ideal scenario. I know it's not always the case for everyone, and I've had the privilege in my education career to move into positions that I felt were advantageous for me and my family and hopefully the schools or groups whom I served. At the same time, if you realize you are not serving others with care, compassion, and determination, take the time to ask why. None of us is ever doing this perfectly. We all have bad days, difficult times, and exasperating moments. When you weigh those against the rewarding ones, however, work is often more rewarding when you see how it is connected to serving and helping others. In other words, your decisions in the work you do will bring you the most joy when your work and your values are intertwined.

2. *Making decisions or transitions in your career should be based on your most important core values.*

The most difficult decisions along a career path often center on how to know if you're making the right choice when you come to a crossroads. Some people I know are comfortable with not considering the pathways in front of them at all; they simply wait for open doors before considering their next moves. Others, particularly those I coach, think seriously and consistently about potential pathways as they project where they want to be in the next year, three years, five years, or ten years.

Any time I have made a transition in my work, the decision has been difficult, not only because of my deep love for the role I was in, but also because I was unsure if the trajectory of my choices would be good for my family or my future, or if they would truly match my personal values. In these scenarios, I made lists of pros and cons. I wrote out a trajectory of where a pathway might take me in one year, three years, five years, or ten years. I considered the pathways I was on at the time and where that might take me over those same periods. Sometimes I came to an impasse, realizing that two pathways were both good ones and could potentially align with my career, family, and core values and keep me connected to what I loved.

In a moment of prayer and reflection, a thought came to me. I don't want to presume that I heard the voice of God, but the impression I received sounded something like this: "Will, I don't care what you do as long as you find your deepest satisfaction in me."

The suggestion was that the right choices result most often when your heart stays in the right place. You may not share the same convictions, but the question in hard decision making remains the same, whether you are a person of faith or not: Where are you finding your deepest satisfaction?

- If your deepest satisfaction is found in your prestige, then you're probably making the wrong decision.
- If your deepest satisfaction is found in your salary, then you're probably making the wrong decision.
- If your deepest satisfaction is found in your achievements or accolades, then you're probably placing your core values in the wrong things.

Where are your deepest satisfactions found? Do you know who you are at your core? Do you know how you can contribute to the betterment of your friends, family, neighbors, and students? If you can answer those questions, I would say you're on the right path, no matter your title, your job description, your salary, or which choice you make. As you consider the pathways in front of you, I want to pose some questions that have helped me stay centered in difficult decisions:

- How would you describe your core values if you had to condense them into one sentence?
- As you step into your day, how do you allow those core values to direct and guide your decisions, thoughts, interactions, and conversations with others?
- When wrestling with difficult decisions, how do you allow those core values to inform your final choices?
- At the end of the day, if you reflect back and cannot see how your core values influenced the work that you've done, what is one thing you can do at that very moment to reconnect with those core values?

These reflections have been crucial for me, not just when considering the difficult choices of pathways and career changes, but also in the small choices that occur every day.

What are Your Greatest Joys?

One of my favorite quotes is from the movie *Chariots of Fire*, when Eric Liddell, the Olympic runner, was preparing for the race in which he would win the gold medal. He said, "I believe God made me for a purpose, but He also made me fast. And when I run, I feel His pleasure."

What are the things that you do that give you the greatest pleasure and joy? It's very possible you were made for those things. As I've stepped through the stages of my education career—teaching, leading, consulting, coaching, providing professional development, and writing books—I've found a lot of joy. But, sometimes, I still wrestle with whether I am making the right choices. Even on my best days, I sometimes become discouraged when I'm not seeing the outcomes I have imagined.

The truth is that almost every journey takes you on a pathway that will include both joys and disappointments. The challenge is in examining the positives and negatives and recognizing that it's not the outcome that defines your value. You are still valuable, and so are the people you serve, regardless of their outcomes. And yet that doesn't change your desire for a better outcome.

Avoiding Imposter Syndrome

Like many others, at times I struggle with the guilt of feeling like I am still lacking in knowledge, expertise, or ability. Who am I to be providing feedback and guidance for others?

A few months ago, I was attending one of my son's high school band events. The directors had organized a community event for the band to perform their fall marching competition for parents and community members. My son's band director, Mr. Chris Harris, was explaining to the community how proud he was of the band's hard work that semester, and yet there was a point in the training of the band members when he realized they were not completely stepping into their full potential. For some reason, they seemed to be holding back from their strongest performance. So, he read them a poem from Marianne Williamson (1992):

> Our deepest fear is not that we are inadequate.
> Our deepest fear is that we are powerful beyond measure.
> It is our light, not our darkness that most frightens us.
> We ask ourselves, 'Who am I to be brilliant, gorgeous, talented, fabulous?' Actually, who are you not to be? You are a child of God.
> Your playing small does not serve the world. There is nothing enlightened about shrinking so that other people won't feel insecure around you.
> We are all meant to shine, as children do.
> We were born to make manifest the glory of God that is within us.
> It's not just in some of us; it's in everyone.
> And as we let our own light shine, we unconsciously give other people permission to do the same.
> As we are liberated from our own fear, our presence automatically liberates others.

One of the best antidotes for imposter syndrome is remembering it is OK to shine. It is a good thing to look for what you love to do and pursue it. The essence of reaching one's full potential is understanding the impact it can have, not just on oneself, but also on those around you.

> **The essence of reaching one's full potential is understanding the impact it can have, not just on oneself, but also on those around you.**

Let's Wrap This Up

One morning, when driving to school with my oldest daughter, I asked her out of curiosity, "What's one of your most memorable moments growing up?"

I expected her to recall vacations we had been on—perhaps hiking in the mountains of Colorado or playing in the sands on the Gulf Shores. Instead, she surprised me by saying, "One of my happiest memories is sitting in the kiddie pool in the backyard with you when I was a toddler, just staring at the clouds and being together."

That moment struck me for its simplicity, but it also reminded me that, at the end of the day, my daughter didn't care about my job title or even remember the grand vacation experiences. What she cherished was the feeling of togetherness and the simple beauty of nature.

Perhaps you don't overthink situations like I do or wrestle with questions of who you are, but I suspect you care deeply about your work and those you serve, or you wouldn't be reading a book like this one. Focus on things that connect you to your core values, remember who you really are, and remember that your work is only important if it means staying true to those values and helping others remember how valuable and loved they are as well.

Time for Reflection

1. What is one of the most cherished moments from your childhood?
2. What are some activities that make you feel pure joy and satisfaction, whether they're connected to work or outside of work?
3. If you had to define yourself without a title or position, or even the label of parent, spouse, or partner, how would you define yourself?

4. As you think about the choices in front of you, how are those choices connected to what you believe is most important for your own development and the development of those around you?
5. How can you be content today with the moment you are in, to make the most of it, since none of us are guaranteed tomorrow?

CHAPTER 14

∽

How Mentoring Others Shapes You, Too

The other morning, I was jogging along a bustling town road just before school with Ivy, my trusty running companion, at my side. As we made our way down a long hill, the scene before me was a parade of cars and buses lined up to drop off students at the local high school. To my right, a grassy bank stretched into the distance, while on my left, four lanes of traffic buzzed with activity, cars darting in and out of the school zone.

It was anything but peaceful. The noise of engines and tires whizzing by, the glint of metal, and the flashing lights in the distance all served as a reminder of the hustle and bustle that comes with the start of a school day. I knew later that morning I'd be attending meetings with educators, discussing strategies with those who were at that moment greeting students and ushering in the day.

As I descended the bank, following the long sidewalk with the grassy hill to my right, something caught my eye. The morning sun cast beams of light that danced upon the dew-covered grass, and each blade glistened with tiny droplets that caught the sunlight like an ocean of sparkling jewels. At that moment, even with the chaos of traffic and the rush of the impending school day, I was captivated by nature's simple beauty found in life's small wonders.

I experience such a mix of emotions on mornings like this. I'm sweating from a morning jog and already thinking about the work ahead, but then I'm reminded of the people I support and the hard work they do.

One day, I was expressing this mix of emotions to a friend of mine who is nearing retirement. I told him I felt guilty that I loved my work so much while supporting educators who were, as I put it, "still in the trenches."

He asked me, "How many years were you a teacher and principal?"

"Twenty-four," I said.

He simply said, "Well, the way I see it, it sounds like it's someone else's turn."

I think sometimes in education, as people progress in their careers, they look toward retirement and think about what life will be like when they step away. Some feel exhilaration at the idea of doing something new, while others, like me, might feel a tinge of guilt knowing the weight that is still being carried by the people we leave behind.

But my friend's words were a good reminder that we are all in different cycles of life. Whatever cycle you are experiencing, you can make the most of it by modeling, mentoring, and preparing others for the work they will be doing, knowing you will not always be in the picture.

The Do's of Mentoring

Mentoring is about demonstrating and showing others ways to perform their work more efficiently, productively, and successfully. How can you intentionally invest in others so that you leave any place better than you found it?

When I was in the classroom, I volunteered several times to take student teachers into my room because I enjoyed the opportunity to mentor and give feedback to young potential teachers. I loved to watch them take on that work themselves—including the highs and lows of lesson planning and instruction.

As a school administrator, I had the privilege of training several assistant principals to be my companion administrators. With each one, I tried to imagine what their first days on the job would be like compared to what mine was like. Instead of just throwing them in the water to "sink or swim," so to speak, I wanted to guide them through a typical day by sitting down and walking through some potential scenarios.

We would take time to schedule observing and evaluating teachers throughout the year. Or we might pretend that we were conducting a student discipline meeting. We would painstakingly walk through what to expect in daily scenarios, from data entry to a difficult conversation—these small details of the work that often become so familiar that we forget it's unfamiliar to newcomers.

Mentoring simply means taking the things that have become second nature to you and teaching others and showing others to do the same. Walking through scenarios with people in advance allows them to sense what their own journey will be like, and hopefully they are better prepared to do it by themselves. No matter how much practice you do, though, there are always scenarios for which you've never been able to prepare. Mentoring also means inviting others to reach out when they need guidance, assistance, or feedback.

> Mentoring simply means taking the things that have become second nature to you and teaching others and showing others to do the same.

The Don'ts of Mentoring

In Michael Bungay Stanier's (2020) second book, *The Advice Trap*, he talks about the challenge of coaching others when you tend to share more advice than is really helpful—and it can be overwhelming for your mentee. A good mentoring relationship provides guidance, modeling, and input, but there is no need to share every single story or piece of information you have in your mind. I've learned this the hard way.

I made this mistake once when a young administrator invited me to dinner to talk through the overwhelming experiences he was having in his first year. Instead of listening deeply and trying to understand exactly what the real challenges were for him, I gave him lots of advice on techniques, tips, and ideas for organizational management and classroom management.

At one point in the conversation, he looked at me and said, "Really, I think you may know too much to help me. What I really need is someone who is still in the work who can tell me how to survive until tomorrow."

I realized at that moment that my advice monster had taken over. What he needed was to be understood, not to be overwhelmed with more information than he could take in during one conversation. When mentoring others, first understand what someone needs and then try to guide them in that direction, knowing when enough is enough.

Doing the Next Thing

Mentoring also means helping others do the next thing. How do you take an overwhelming amount of information or tasks and narrow them down to the next best steps? I've discovered that, once you've expressed the real challenge for what you want to accomplish, the most important thing to do next is simply decide what the next step is.

As a mentor to others, it's crucial to avoid the trap of oversharing ideas and suggestions. Instead, narrow the focus to what is the most important challenge at hand. Then help others determine their next step.

Author Cale Birk, another guest on my podcast, calls this the *impact question*: What would be the observable impact of taking this action? Cale's advice is that when we understand the impact a decision is having on student learning, teacher development, or community relations, we better understand which decision to make that will most directly influence the outcomes we desire (Parker, 2023).

The Chapter You're In

Whenever you are in a mentoring relationship, whether with students, educators, or others, it is important not to become overwhelmed by what has yet to develop in the person you are helping.

One year, a school counselor and I were advising a high school student who was struggling with academics but also had a substance addiction. While partnering with his family, we managed to find him resources and in-patient treatment that helped him take the next steps toward recovery and achievement. At that moment, we felt so proud of him and ourselves. Sadly, a year later, we found ourselves in another conversation with him after he had relapsed. We had to identify a new pathway with him, this time alone, as he was now estranged from his family. A year later, he was clean, had graduated, and was enlisted in the military.

One day, after another conversation with the same student, I turned to my counselor friend and said, "Wow, each chapter with this student brings a different set of challenges and obstacles. I'm glad I was around long enough to enjoy this chapter."

When working with others, you have a unique look into whatever chapter of life they are currently experiencing. You cannot rewind the clock or push fast forward. You must be present for whatever chapter you are in. Just as you cannot see your own blind spots or limitations, others may not be aware of their own objective reality at times. Be patient with them, and be patient with yourself. Treat others as you would want to be treated when navigating difficult pathways, and you may find more grace for the pathways you are navigating yourself.

Let Mentors Shape You

Don't believe the false assumption that you're the smartest person in the room. A good mentoring relationship is one in which the mentor is learning right alongside the mentee. Whenever I'm working with someone who is tackling a big challenge, I remind myself that this is a complex issue from which I may learn as much as the person who has asked for my guidance or input.

Like a good teacher, be willing to slow down your own lessons and become curious about the questions others are having while learning. Each time you ask for their input, you are inviting an opportunity to be surprised by something you might not have considered before.

The same truth applies to all relationships. The person you are reflecting with will often illuminate a truth, insight, author, resource, or application that you had not considered before. Let these moments shape you as much as you hope to shape those whom you are helping.

Letting Go

One of the toughest moments in my career was when I had been named the incoming high school principal. One day, the retiring principal, Donna Brogan, pulled me aside one day at the end of school. "Will, you need to know I have banked enough sick days that when graduation ends, I'm taking off the rest of my contract days. I want to spend this time with my family, and I believe you are in good shape to close out the school year."

HOW MENTORING OTHERS SHAPES YOU, TOO

I was terrified. Not only would I be managing the end of a school year, with teachers checking out, grades being finalized and reported, and reports going out, but I would also be replacing my own vacated position at the same time by hiring a new assistant principal. I remember feeling like I did as a first-year teacher—almost paralyzed by the expectations and lists of to-dos.

Looking back, however, I realize what a gift Donna gave me. She trusted me, and she was willing to let go. She had spent years mentoring me, guiding me, and coaching me in my own leadership development. She knew I would rise to the task. The day after graduation, I woke up early and went for a morning run. During that time, I asked myself: What have I done in past situations where I have felt overwhelmed that has helped me move forward with success?

I remembered what it was like being a new teacher and a new assistant principal. During those times, I learned to make lists of all my expected activities. I learned the hard way to reach out and ask others for their input and help. After my run, I drove to school and gathered my office team, and I told them I was overwhelmed and wanted their help. Together we made a list of all the to-dos involved in closing out the year. We delegated tasks, made an inventory list of teachers, and began doing the next thing and then the next thing.

Over the years, I have rinsed and repeated that method for collaborating around difficult tasks. I have also learned to value the importance of letting go. When you have mentored others, they deserve the trust and confidence to do the next thing without you having to be present.

It may seem counterintuitive that your work as an educator is to equip others to do the hard work without you—even the work of being in the trenches when the day comes for you to pack it up, go home for a long jog, and remember that it's someone else's turn.

Time for Reflection

1. What skills do you possess that may be valuable in helping others develop these as skills of their own?
2. In what ways are you being intentional in developing the capacity of others?
3. What are some practical how-to's that would be helpful for you to write down for someone learning a new task or responsibility?
4. Where in your schedule do you prioritize mentoring others?
5. Who may be going through a difficult "chapter of their life"? Where can you make a difference, and what controls do you have to let go?

CHAPTER 15

Imagination Multiplied to Work and Life

When I was growing up in a rural area of west Tennessee as a boy, my life was pretty simple—at least to my perspective. If I wanted to visit family or friends who lived down the road, I would either have to walk a mile to the nearest home or ride my bike down gravel roads to see them. None of my family members locked the doors on their houses, which meant I could go visit and let myself in at my grandparents' or aunts' and uncles' homes any time I wanted.

During high school, my father reenlisted in the Navy, and we moved to New York. He was first stationed in Brooklyn in the shipyard, and we lived for a few days in an apartment provided by the U.S. Navy until we secured housing in East Meadows, New York, a suburb on Long Island.

My eyes were opened to the differences in the lives of new neighbors and friends, many of whom were from New York, but also many had lived in other cities and states as part of military families. I was surprised the first time a friend asked permission for me to come over.

WHOSE PERMISSION ARE YOU WAITING FOR?

Where I grew up, no permission was needed, as we came over unannounced at any time.

My world expanded even more when I went to college one summer, and I had the opportunity to travel to Central America. This was my first time in any cross-cultural setting where I was the minority among the majority Hispanic population. Suddenly, my limited perspectives seemed to be growing globally.

When I became a teacher, like most new teachers, my idea of what it meant to teach was limited to my experiences as a student in primary school, high school, and what I had learned in college. My views of education began to expand from theoretical to practical the more I interacted with other educators within my own district or met other educators across my state.

I began to ask, "How can I expand learning for students?" or "How can an entire school see improvement?" These questions took on different meanings when I connected them to the context of others and their experiences.

Whether I discovered new ideas by reading books, attending conferences, listening to podcasts, or going on tours of other schools, each interaction, each day, and each year expanded my thinking and gave me the opportunity to imagine possibilities beyond my own limited experience.

Thinking Bigger than You've Imagined Before

You probably have your own stories of when the world opened to you in new ways. In the spirit of good teaching, I would like to ask you a few reflective questions:

1. Could you be expanding your work in ways you have never imagined?
2. What if you could see growth ten times your current understanding and outcomes in just one year?

IMAGINATION MULTIPLIED TO WORK AND LIFE

If that second question makes you uncomfortable, welcome to an invitation to multiply your imagination.

In Dan Sullivan and Dr. Benjamin Hardy's (2023) book *10x Is Easier Than 2x: How World Class Entrepreneurs Achieve More by Doing Less*, Sullivan shares lessons from the executive coaching he has been providing for almost fifty years. One of the most important exercises he does with business leaders is to ask them to imagine—not how they want to grow their business twice as big as it currently is—but how to increase their growth ten times their current status.

Something happens when you're pushed to imagine growth beyond anything that you are personally capable of accomplishing in your present state. We do this naturally in the progress of learning over time, and it can be transformational to imagine growth in ways bigger than you are comfortable considering. Here are three implications of imagining 10x possibilities:

1. *When you imagine 10x growth, you are suddenly inviting ideas for growth that take you to places you've never imagined.*

    Think about one area of your life where you'd like to see improvement. Let's choose health and nutrition as an example. What if, instead of making a few changes in your activities and food choices, you embraced an approach that could produce healthier outcomes ten times your current condition? What if you could be ten times healthier at the end of one year than you are now?

    Immediately, you probably feel uncomfortable about the amount of effort, focus, and discipline this would require. Something else happens as well if you give yourself permission to imagine it as a possibility, though: you begin considering action steps, systems, and changes you may not have ever considered before.

2. *Try 10x thinking in such a large perspective change that it almost requires you to invite others into the process.*

Because thinking so imaginatively takes you far beyond your comfort zone, you quickly realize 10x outcomes almost always require asking others for input, advice, resources, or help in some manner. If you were able to accomplish it alone, it is likely not a true 10x goal.

3. *If you are willing to imagine all the ramifications of a 10x growth possibility, you are required to focus only on the skills that are your greatest strengths.*

According to Sullivan and Hardy (2023), businesses achieve true growth through only twenty percent of the actions a leader takes during their workday. What would happen if, instead, you were able to delegate those other tasks and concentrate eighty percent of your efforts on tasks that directly lead to significant improvements?

Does that sound too good to be true? It is for the people who are content with focusing twenty percent of their time and expertise on tasks most important to them. For those willing to flip the percentages, the ramifications compel you to consider new ideas and actions you may have never taken before.

Imagine the Possibilities

Here is another mindset challenge: Imagine for a moment where you would like to grow in your own learning experiences, student outcomes, or career over the next year, three years, five years, or even ten years. Now, imagine if the growth you would like to experience within the next ten years could actually be experienced in one year.

1. What would those ten-year outcomes look like if you were able to achieve them within the next twelve months?
2. What drastic actions would you have to take?
3. What collaboration would be involved?
4. What resources would you need to employ?

5. What learning would need to take place for you to reach a ten-year mark within the next year?

Any time you are willing to think about growth in exponential terms, you recognize the necessity of determination and the limitations of your own capabilities at the same time.

If I look at the trajectory of my career, I have achieved 10x growth in terms of influence and outcomes over the past three decades. For example, when I decided to launch Principal Matters, LLC, in 2023, I set goals to dramatically increase my offerings, secure stronger financial earnings, and practice intentional generosity. Thinking about this kind of multiplied growth required me to think strategically. I had to consider practical questions:

- What are my core values, and how do my offerings match those values?
- In what ways am I structuring my work so that I have time to do what I am best at doing and find joy in the process?
- How many clients will I need for exponential growth?
- How many dates for training sessions would I need to secure?
- How many contracts would I need to sign by January, February, March, and so on?
- How much content would I need to increase or redesign?
- What responsibilities and tasks would I need to delegate by hiring someone to help me achieve those goals?

A Case Study in Imagination Multiplied

Let's take another example of an assistant principal who is looking at the possibility of stepping into a head principal role within the next two to five years. They know the common pathway that leadership step requires:

- Gaining experience as a leader,
- Building a track record of success,
- Maintaining the trust of colleagues,
- Identifying potential openings,
- Interviewing for those openings,
- Discovering they are the right fit,
- Being invited to join the team, and
- Stepping into that role.

Because fewer leadership openings exist than other positions within schools, these roles are more competitive and require advanced degrees and more experience. However, they often offer higher compensation, as principals typically work twelve-month contracts compared to teachers who take off for typical school breaks. Now, imagine that the same assistant principal envisions growth far beyond just becoming a principal:

- They begin to see themselves as a leader whose influence can make a difference across the entire district, not just within the school they would be assigned to as a principal.
- They gather input from those leading in the capacities they aspire to, perhaps seeking conversations with assistant superintendents, directors, or superintendents to discover what they value most in the principals leading their schools.
- They might also engage with business or corporate leaders in settings where growth and expansion are a normal part of the company, recognizing that some of these strategies can be applied to a school setting.
- While waiting for a principal position to open, this leader might start writing articles about what they are learning in education and contribute to journals, educational magazines, or websites dedicated to education leadership.

- By doing so, they develop a reputation as a leader in their field. Suddenly, this leader is recognized by peers and is invited to present to aspiring leaders or fellow leaders at state principals conferences or workshops.
- Perhaps their growth is noticed to the point where they are nominated for an award by someone within their district.

What I just described is the process I have seen high-achieving educators apply for accelerating opportunities. By the time these leaders move into new roles or responsibilities, they have not waited for the new job title or position to pursue the personal and professional growth needed for the next level. Because they think expansively about their growth and look far beyond the next year, the next three years, or the next five years, they engage in activities that expand their experience and understanding, which prepares them for their future roles and responsibilities.

Whether you are a teacher, administrator, professor, or student, the same mindset shift applies to how you want to grow. Are you willing to imagine the possibilities beyond incremental growth, expand your thinking exponentially, and then take bold action toward that end?

Impacts on Individuals and Systems

While writing this chapter, I reached out to an education leader, Amy Nall, who is the assistant superintendent for the Archdiocese of Louisville Catholic Schools in Louisville, Kentucky. I've worked with her and leaders from those schools for the last few years. Amy is an accomplished, veteran educator. I wanted to ask her to engage in an activity with me. First, I asked her to imagine two times the growth that principals across their forty-eight schools might achieve. When I posed the question about doubling growth, she talked about the following ideas:

- In order to double growth, she would imagine their schools retaining leaders year to year.
- More teacher leaders and assistant principals would be recruited and trained for ongoing growth.
- Assistant principals, in particular, would develop deeper knowledge, higher degrees, and more training to take on responsibilities and leadership in the years ahead.
- They would scaffold their onboarding process to increase leader expertise. This way, the individual growth of their leaders could meet the capacity needed for the kind of student achievement they wanted to experience.

These were great responses, but I wanted to go deeper. Next, I asked her to imagine what would be necessary for stronger outcomes for her leaders if those outcomes could be experienced ten times what they are presently. What kinds of robust actions would have to be taken? Here she paused for a long time. Then she responded as follows:

- The entire system would need stronger enrollment efforts if their schools were to match the kind of stellar results that these kinds of leaders and their schools would be exhibiting with 10x growth.
- With 10x growth, outcomes should have little or no disparity between more affluent communities and less affluent communities. Every school needed robust resources that may not be presently available.
- With 10x growth, tuition costs and funding dollars should be made available for any constituent interested in applying for their schools. Now, there are limits on who can apply, often based on sustainability and affordability.

Can you see the differences comparing a 2x growth model to a 10x growth model? Both practices were valuable, but the 10x model expanded from growing the individual strengths of leaders to improving the capacity of the entire system—recognizing that, if results were ten times as strong, then robust growth and systemic changes would be inevitable. This kind of practice takes us outside the normal predictable possibilities of what happens when we try to grow from year to year and leads us into often disruptive but exciting possibilities.

Your Limits Invite Collaboration

At the age of sixty, competitive swimmer Diana Nyad decided to achieve a world record that no man or woman had ever set: to swim from the island of Cuba to the coast of Florida, a 102-mile trek through jellyfish- and shark-infested waters, with changing flows and ebbs in the tides. Her first attempt, after two years of training, was a failure. After she was stung severely by jellyfish, she had to give up the swim. But two years later, when she attempted the feat again, she achieved it.

When she stood on the shore and was asked by the press how she achieved this feat, she said two things: "Never give up" and "Teamwork." Later, in a famous TED Talk, she described why she said those two things. She explained that, in her first attempt at achieving that world record, she relied upon her strength, but not as expansively upon others.

The second time she achieved the goal, she recognized that the only way someone could break that world record was to surround themselves with boats of specialists in navigation, nutrition, and health, all watching out for dangers coming in the waters ahead. She was still a solitary swimmer who achieved this goal, yet she did it by leaning into the strengths of the teams of people surrounding her (Nyad, 2013).

Let's face it. No matter your gifts, if you want to see 10x growth, your capabilities will be limited by your strengths, skills, and experiences.

The good news is that you will be forced to collaborate with, connect with, or depend on others to combine their strengths with yours and reach extraordinary outcomes.

A Word of Caution

As with every lesson in this book, I feel compelled to add a word of caution as we wrap up this chapter. I have a love/hate relationship with self-help books. On the one hand, I appreciate being pushed to think outside the box. On the other hand, I realize many of the principles involved in these practices make assumptions about time, place, and context that vary from person to person.

Applying an imaginative multiplication to your own goals and aspirations is meant to encourage you to stretch beyond the boundaries of what is often termed as "normal" or "ordinary." Words like *normal* and *ordinary* are not bad words as long as they are not self-imposed or externally imposed limits on your potential.

At the same time, your abilities to reach extraordinary goals are a combination of both personal achievement and profound privileges afforded by time and place. No matter how hard anyone works, they cannot control where they are born or force the skies to produce rain clouds across drought-stricken landscapes.

Your ability to dream big is a gift. If, however, the goal of an imagination multiplication exercise is only applied for selfish gain or the simple thrill of spurring imagination, then the limits on this practice will be as shallow as any other self-serving strategy. But if you give yourself permission to dream beyond the ordinary—even allowing yourself to think multiple times beyond the experiences or outcomes you would normally envision while applying this practice to the potential benefit of those whom you are serving–then you will find a satisfaction much greater than any self-help practice can offer.

Will you give yourself permission to dream big if the results increase help for others? Will you allow yourself to imagine those possibilities on a scale ten times what you normally allow yourself to dream? If you do, you may, as the saying goes, still land among the stars.

Time for Reflection

1. If you could envision a future that is ten times greater in outcome and influence than you are presently experiencing, how would you describe that future?
2. What steps or actions may be required to move toward fulfilling goals that are ten times what you would normally set for your personal or professional growth?
3. Whose expertise, input, or collaboration would you need to seek in order to reach goals ten times larger than normal?
4. What kind of courage would be required to move in the direction of 10x growth? What permission would you need to give yourself in order to say yes to necessary actions?

CHAPTER 16

Backward Mapping for Reaching Goals

The first time I hiked the western coastal path of Wales in 2022, my wife and I took a train from Aberystwyth, Wales, to the town of Borth. From there we hiked seven miles southward back along the coast toward the university town where our daughter, Katie, attended. Along the trail we met a retired professor from Cardiff University, and he shared with us a story of a Celtic ritual he followed each morning. On his walks, he placed a piece of wood on the beach south of the path that faced the setting sun. The northern side of the pathway where he lived near Borth was far enough inland that, at that time of the year, the cliffs blocked him from seeing the sun setting into the ocean each night.

The tradition, according to his story, was that each morning ancient coastal dwellers placed a stick of wood on the southern beach where the setting sun was currently visible each evening until late spring. By late spring, the position of the sun would change enough that it would become visible from his dwelling further north on the coastland.

When the sunset disappeared from the southern beach, he and others would return there and light a fire from all the wood placed there. The fire was a way to mark the departure of the setting sun from that part of the coastal path. It was also an omen to remind the sun where it should return that time next year. Although I am confident the sun would still be rising on the coastal path near Borth without this ritual, I like the simple reminder that for centuries people have planned in advance for the outcomes they hope will come to them.

Just like our newfound friend on the coastal path and other dwellers for hundreds or thousands of years, if you know the end result you want to reach, you take the necessary steps toward that end.

Beginning with the End in Mind

As you think about important decisions and pathways of your own, I want to give some very practical feedback about mapping out your plans and strategies. Backward mapping is a term I learned from a friend and retired principal, Dave Sandowich, who was the principal of Haddon Heights High School in Haddon Heights, New Jersey, for twenty-one years. As a veteran leader, as well as an avid sailboat enthusiast, Dave often applies his lessons in sea navigation and planning ocean journeys to school leadership.

In the summer of 2019, Dave invited me to sail with him off the coast of Kent Island, Maryland, where he and his wife now live. As we were enjoying the expanse of blue sky and the whip of wind along his sails, Dave shared with me how difficult it can be to sail upwind—driving into the wind instead of going along with its natural flow. He later explained this same concept to me in a subsequent podcast interview, saying:

> Some sailors will not want to do all that work and never sail to a destination that is upwind. Leadership is like that. It would be nice to just set a worthy objective point for the organization in that direction and arrive in a reasonable amount of time. . . .

You must commit to the end destination and work your way toward it, often headed in what seems to be away from your mark. You realize that it will take more time, but you will see progress made.

Feedback will be essential as you adjust, regroup, and keep moving. As in sailing . . . it takes a skill set, and the more experience you have and the more often you do it, the results come easier. (Parker, 2019)

Most educators understand the importance of backward mapping when applied to both their own education journey and building curriculum for the results they want to see in student learning. Each year teachers map out curriculum and lesson plans for an entire school year. Airlines map out routes, destinations, dates, and fares. Entire industries are dedicated to the supply chain routes necessary for delivering goods around the globe.

If we know these systems work in teaching, business development, and industry, how can you apply the same principle to mapping outcomes for doing what you love? It requires intentional planning, scheduling, and execution.

When I made the decision to leave my position as executive director for my state secondary principal association, for instance, I created one schedule for closing out my responsibilities over an eight-month period, November 1 through June 30. I also created a schedule for the tasks of launching and monetizing my new venture with Principal Matters, LLC.

As an example, here is what my map looked like from the beginning of my to-do's in November until my last official contract date with the association at the end of June. The key was to start at the end and work my way back to the start.

Principal Matters Timeline for Transition with Recommended Actions
(Departure Map and Launching Map)

November

- Meet with key leadership and draft a letter and timeline for departure.

December

- Share the transition announcement and plans with team members, executive committees, and relevant members by December 1.
- Reach out to various contacts with news.
- Create an end-of-year post to share news with listeners.
- Create opening, mid-show, and closing comments for future shows.
- Create a map for launching the new business and draft an ideal schedule for the upcoming year.

January

Association To-Do's:
- Post/advertise the position.
- Submit articles for the February edition.
- Set calendars for the upcoming year.
- Attend and assist at the legislative conference.
- Prepare for the conference.

Commitments:
- Various coaching sessions and Zoom meetings throughout the month.
- Attend mastermind and growth sessions.

Principal Matters To-Do's:
- Set up meetings to discuss options for the upcoming year.
- Follow up with various contacts about retreats, conferences, and collaborations.
- Create applications and manage meetings/requests.
- Research insurance and retirement account options.
- Explore speaker requests for presentations.
- Set up podcast interviews and writing time for book ideas.
- Purchase a new laptop and set up a new office area.
- Conduct a spending/budget audit.

February

Association To-Do's:
- Give an update at the executive committee meeting.
- Begin conducting interviews.
- Begin the legislative session.
- Attend and assist at the conference.
- Plan for the summer conference.
- Attend the second session with a key contact.

Principal Matters Commitments:
- Attend various coaching sessions and Zoom meetings throughout the month.
- Attend mastermind and growth sessions.
- Follow up on proposals and calendar recommendations.
- Update the website with new headshots and changes.

March

Association To-Do's:
- Continue the interview process.
- Submit scholarship applications.

- Attend various conferences and sessions.
- Plan for the summer conference.
- Attend a key advocacy conference.
- Plan for the principal day at the Capitol.

Principal Matters Commitments:
- Attend various coaching sessions and Zoom meetings throughout the month.
- Attend mastermind and growth sessions.
- Travel for a keynote speech and conference attendance.
- Follow up on proposals and calendar recommendations.

April

Association To-Do's:
- Select a candidate by April.
- Attend various conferences and planning sessions.
- Pack up the office and move archived materials.

Principal Matters Commitments:
- Attend various coaching sessions and Zoom meetings throughout the month.
- Attend mastermind and growth sessions.
- Follow up on proposals and calendar recommendations.

May

Association To-Do's:
- Present the new hire at the executive committee meeting.
- Plan for the summer leadership conference.
- Conduct student scholarship interviews.
- Hold transition/training meetings with the new director.

Principal Matters Commitments:
- Attend various coaching sessions and Zoom meetings throughout the month.
- Attend mastermind and growth sessions.
- Follow up on proposals and calendar recommendations.

June

Association To-Do's:
- Attend the summer conference.
- Introduce the new director at summer business meetings.
- Hold transition/training meetings with the new director.

Committees/Teams Participation:
- Participate in various committees and advisory groups.
- Conduct training and consulting for the new director.
- Attend region meetings and provide updates.

Although this plan summarized one backward mapping activity I used in real life, the same process can work for almost any scenario. Achieving the end result requires beginning with the end in mind and working your way backward to the present.

Studying Abroad Example

My wife and I have four children. When our third daughter announced she wanted to attend university overseas, we thought she was joking. She was in her junior year of high school when the COVID-19 pandemic essentially shut down the world, and her research for potential colleges moved into virtual spaces, where she began exploring options that did not require an in-person visit.

At first, I thought I would discourage the idea with a practical assignment. I asked her to create a spreadsheet showing the tuition, costs, and expenses for her top college choices in our state and compare those to the universities she was exploring across the United Kingdom, where she had the most interest.

She returned with a spreadsheet showing me the costs, and I was surprised. Her top three choices in the United Kingdom were either comparable or more affordable than the ones we had been exploring closer to home. Fast forward two years, and she was accepted into Aberystwyth University on the west coast of Wales. She obtained her passport, student visa, housing, insurance coverage, and travel plans.

What began as a dream was actually becoming a reality, but it didn't happen overnight. Her ability to arrive in time for student orientation and classes in her first fall semester began more than two years before when she identified her destination and then worked her way backward in order to prioritize, apply, take action, and schedule every detail in advance of the final destination.

In the summer of 2024, we took our entire family to Wales for Katie's graduation. Our first night there, we stood on the same coastal walk we visited two years earlier that runs along the seafront on the west coast facing Cardigan Bay. The beach is covered in pebbles, rounded smooth over centuries of tidal waves—black, white, brown, red, and some mixed-in swirls of these colors. I stood back and took in the scene. Each family member was scouring the shores for rocks, taking photos of waves hitting the shoreline, and gazing off into the horizon as the setting sun cast hues of blues and purples onto the placid Atlantic waters.

If you had asked me in 2020, when Katie headed to Aberystwyth University, whether I had imagined experiencing this specific moment in advance, the truth is I had not. Katie, however, had imagined it, and her backward mapping made it possible for her to achieve that dream.

What is something extraordinary you dream of achieving? Perhaps it is growth in your own career. Maybe it is traveling to a new destination. Do you want to achieve a new certification or degree? Do you want to work in a new role or take on a new responsibility? Or maybe you want to map out what you would like to do in retirement and work your way backward from there.

Whatever it is, you can move toward achieving that dream by imagining the end result, setting specific tasks and dates for its achievement, and backward mapping your way into that reality.

The Joy in the Journey

In the summer 2024 Wimbledon tennis match, Spain's Carlos Alcaraz bested Serbia's Novak Djokovic. Afterward, both men gave remarks to the waiting crowd. Although Djokovic lost, this was his tenth time to compete in the championship. Just a few weeks earlier, he had undergone knee surgery.

His comeback was not strong enough to win, but his competitive spirit was inspiring. As he addressed the crowd, he also acknowledged that his son was learning tennis and he was coaching him. "I don't know if I have the nerve to keep going with my coaching career with my son. There are a lot of beautiful things in life, Son. Tennis is not the only thing, but if you really wish to pursue it, I'll be there for you," he said, with emotion in his voice.

As I watched Djokovic giving this speech on TV, I was struck by the fact that his speech was so inspiring, even though he had lost the match.

Backward planning is no guarantee to reach a destination or a goal. Disappointments in planning ahead are just as much a reality as reaching goals, and sometimes the failures are more likely. The simple truth, however, is that you are more likely to reach goals with specific plans, deadlines, and checklists than simply hoping for a better outcome with no plan in place for moving forward. At the same time, do not allow your planning to keep you from being in the moment and relishing the gift of the day, time, place, and people with you right now.

One more memory from my daughter Katie: When she was making her plans to leave home and study abroad, we were driving together in our neighborhood. She said to me, "Dad, I have so many teachers who grew up in this town and said they dreamed of living somewhere else but never had the courage to try. I don't want to be forty years old someday and be the person regretting that I never tried."

> You are more likely to reach goals with specific plans, deadlines, and checklists than simply hoping for a better outcome with no plan in place for moving forward.

Four years later, she reached the destination of the backward mapping it took to reach this important milestone. I have been inspired by her courage, and I would have been just as proud had she not reached her goals. May you have courage today to think deeply about the goals, destinations, and outcomes you want to achieve in your life, family, work or school—no matter the outcomes.

Time for Reflection

1. Name a destination, outcome, or goal you really want to accomplish. This could be a year, three years, five years, or ten years from now. The time is up to you. What is that goal or outcome?
2. If you could set a specific date for reaching that goal, destination, or outcome, what is that date?
3. In order to reach that specific deadline, make a list of as many actions you can think of to see this happen. As you create this list, keep in mind the following:
    + Who are the people you would need to involve in pursuing this pathway?

BACKWARD MAPPING FOR REACHING GOALS

- What resources would you need to have available to accomplish this goal?
- What difficult choices or decisions would need to be made in advance and when?
- What benchmarks along the way would you need to accomplish the appropriate steps?
- What false assumptions or unnecessary barriers would you need to eliminate?

4. Based on the above, what specific tasks and deadlines do you need to schedule between now and then to accomplish each task or action you've identified?

CHAPTER 17

Scaling Your Influence

I grew up in a family that regularly attended church, and some of my earliest memories include sitting around a table with other toddler-aged children listening to lessons from my Sunday school teacher. In the New Testament scriptures, Jesus tells a story of a farmer. According to the parable, a profitable farmer plans to build bigger barns to hold the increased production of his profits, not realizing that that very night he would die. He should have been paying attention to those things in life more important than growing wealthier. Jesus finishes the passage by asking, "What does it profit a man to gain the whole world and lose his own soul?"

That story stood out to me as a child because my grandfather was a farmer. Storing up goods for winter was a good choice. Storing up more than you need—or in the wrong ways—might lead to other problems. For instance, when farmers do not allow their hay to dry before baling or rolling it, those "green bales" can actually self-combust in a hot barn. An impatient or unwise farmer can burn down his barn when he stores hay before it is dry enough.

Scaling is meant to lead to growth in profits—a good motivation but not the most important. We live in a time and place that is both unique and challenging at the same time. On the one hand, technology connects us within seconds to people across the world. We can board a plane and, within twenty-four hours, disembark on the other side of the world. On the other hand, time has not changed our desire to want more—people spend a lot of time and energy pursuing what they believe will bring them fulfillment.

> If reaching your ultimate goals in life becomes the driving motivation for why you exist, you will find yourself disappointed.

If reaching your ultimate goals in life becomes the driving motivation for why you exist, you will find yourself disappointed. The truer rewards of life, namely the ones that come through deeper, meaningful relationships, always lead to a better treasure. In other words, if the outcomes of growing your influence are not for the mutual benefit of others, then you're filling your barn in vain.

Having said that, what does it mean to scale your influence, and how is it an important part of thinking about your pathway and future? In business, the idea of scaling is taking an existing trajectory of productivity or profit and creating systems that increase those outcomes. "All ships rise with a tide" is a common phrase we hear when being encouraged to not be selfish with our growth, knowledge, or resources.

During your lifetime, you will gain knowledge, skills, and experiences that allow you growth and improvement. What you do with the benefits of that growth—your strategy for scaling influence in the best possible ways—requires as much intentionality as any other goal, plan, or system you design, execute, or achieve.

So, what do I mean, then, by scaling your influence? For me, scaling growth means expanding and maximizing the opportunities for others to grow alongside you—and ultimately on their own.

Let me share an example. During my years in education, I have taught or worked alongside thousands of students, teachers, leaders, and community members. Each one of them has offered a unique gift to me in their own ways. I have also learned that, when I stay connected to others, invest in their growth, or invite them to ongoing learning, something always happens that benefits me as well. As I engage with them in their growth, I continue to learn and grow as well.

Sometimes those benefits come as new knowledge. Sometimes they come as opportunities to experience new places. Sometimes they result in new income opportunities. Although investing in the growth of others does not always result in these kinds of tangible experiences, I believe that the more we work trying to help others, the more we see growth for ourselves.

When I launched the *Principal Matters* podcast in 2016, I worked alone for the first two years before inviting anyone on the show as a guest. Since then, hundreds of guests have joined me. Every relationship leaves me richer with knowledge, inspiration, and ideas for taking action.

In 2023, when I decided to begin Principal Matters, LLC, as my full-time work, I reached out to several of the leaders I had met through my work and asked them to become Principal Matters Associates. These leaders contributed articles for the weekly newsletter that we shared with subscribers. Many of my associates are fellow authors or presenters, and we refer inquiries to one another when people are looking for resources or professional development help.

Last year, we made it a goal to build a new professional development offering that matched several Principal Matters Associates and their own books or presentations with groups looking to expand their learning for aspiring or newer leaders. This effort resulted in an offer from SAANYS, a principal association in New York, to offer monthly virtual meetings for leaders across the state. Each month, I facilitate the meeting and bring a different associate with me to provide professional learning.

This scaling was a result of multiplying the influence from an entire team of leaders to the growth of newer leaders across an entire state. Everyone benefits, as the presenters sharpen their own skills when passing along their knowledge and expertise, and the listeners become learners who gain valuable wisdom and insights from more experienced educators.

As you grow in your own profession, you have opportunities to scale your influence by investing in others as well. Just remember three simple ideas:

1. *Everyone is an expert in something.*

I have talked before about the power of curiosity, and when it comes to scaling your influence, it begins with the relationships you have with others and your willingness to see the value they bring.

In a recent episode of the *Hidden Brain* podcast, the host Shankar Vendantum interviews Nicholas Epley, a professor at the University of Chicago Booth School of Business. Epley is an expert in social cognition and studies how people perceive other people. In the interview, Epley explains that research confirms most people are hesitant to open up to others or probe deeply in our questions with others because of a fear of being rejected or a fear that we are annoying others with our curiosity. The same research shows, however, that the perceptions are actually opposite of what is actually true.

Most people discover an enormous sense of gratitude when others ask about them and want to know the lessons they have learned or the unique insights they have in their lives or work. When you take time to ask deeper questions of others it benefits you as well—with increases in your own attitude and feelings of well-being (Vendantum, 2023).

I recently put this lesson to the test when sitting on a flight home after two days of presenting professional learning to a group of educators in Louisville, Kentucky. On the connecting flight to Chicago, the man beside me appeared a few years younger than me. Like me, he seemed like someone returning home from business. When I asked him where he was going, we began a conversation that lasted until the plane took off.

For the next twenty minutes or so, I learned about his past working in the field of aviation, his current work in sales for a manufacturing company, and I learned about the lives of his adult children. Surprisingly, he has an adult daughter whose profession as an air traffic controller is the field my youngest son is currently pursuing through his college education. He gave me some tips for my son that I passed along when I arrived home.

The conversation of that flight is embedded in my memory as the result of taking action on the suggestion to stay curious about the people around me. If you're curious enough to inquire, you will learn that everyone is an expert in something that would help you and others grow in knowledge and effectiveness.

2. *Ask how you can help promote the work of others.*

You might be surprised by the reaction you receive from this question, but when you meet someone within your own field, you may be able to introduce them to someone else or to resources that could enhance their growth. Likewise, they may provide you with the same benefits.

More than ten years ago, a friend from church who is also an attorney asked me if I had ever read the work of Dr. Tim Elmore. I had not, so she sent me a link to his website. I soon discovered Dr. Elmore was the CEO of Growing Leaders, an organization based in Atlanta, Georgia, providing curricula to schools about bridging the generation gaps and equipping young people with stronger values and habits for success in school and life.

I emailed Dr. Elmore a quick introduction and asked him what ways I could help support his work. He agreed to be a guest on a series of blog posts I was writing at the time on leadership. Later, Tim was attending an event where I live in Tulsa, Oklahoma, and he reached out with an invitation to dinner. That dinner led to an invitation to an event he was hosting in Atlanta, which I attended compliments of

Growing Leaders. This event led to an invitation the next year for me to present at another event Growing Leaders was hosting.

Fast forward to today, and Dr. Elmore and I remain committed friends. He has been a guest on my podcast two times, we have collaborated at education conferences, and he has continued to include me in invitations to the work Growing Leaders is doing. My one email a decade ago asking him how I could promote his work has resulted in more opportunities for learning than I can count. Tim Elmore has been a mentor to me as an author, a business developer, and a leader.

In 2023, the Maxwell Leadership company purchased Growing Leaders as a division of its work with schools and younger leaders. Dr. Elmore knows something about scaling influence, and he takes time to do so with younger leaders as well as experienced ones.

3. *Trust others to grow and develop without an immediate return on your time invested with them.*

The virtual offering in New York began as an idea more than a year ago. I reached out to twelve leaders in my field and asked them to collaborate around a new offering I wanted to provide for listeners to my podcast or organizations seeking professional development. Ten of those friends agreed to participate, and we created a shared Google Doc where each of us placed our bios and descriptions of our favorite or most popular presentation.

I took these submissions and edited them into a document I created in Canva with speaker photos, titles, and presentation offerings. I began sharing this offering with districts or schools interested in my own presentations. For six months, no one seemed interested in the collaborative work, but I kept showing it to others, and eventually a group in New York offered an opportunity to bring six of my associates along with myself into a virtual offering series for a group of more than fifty education leaders.

Sometimes, taking time to grow with others gives you an immediate sense of satisfaction. At other times, those seeds stay under the surface. You do not always know when they will sprout and bear fruit. The joy, however, in trusting others to grow and develop—whether or not it benefits you—results from the strength it creates to simply know others and learn from their experiences. Just like a good gardener knows, over time, these seeds you plant seem to grow when given the right conditions for growth.

> Sometimes, taking time to grow with others gives you an immediate sense of satisfaction. At other times, those seeds stay under the surface. You do not always know when they will sprout and bear fruit.

Let's Wrap This Up

In the book *The 5 Voices* by Jeremie Kubicek and Steve Cochran, the authors teach that most people have voices that make them uniquely different from others. They take the most common voices found in teams or organizations and break them into five basic types (Cochran & Kubicek, 2016):

- *Pioneers:* champions of vision and trailblazers
- *Guardians:* protectors of resources and inquisitors
- *Connectors:* people who thrive by joining people and resources
- *Nurturers:* those committed to harmony in relationships
- *Creatives:* dreamers and innovators always moving forward

When I take the survey that comes with the book, I rank highest as a connector. Not everyone is comfortable with being a connector.

Connectors love the pursuit of networking, placing others in rooms together, and finding ways to collaborate for solutions. Connectors are also storytellers, and they make really good salespeople.

When I think about the concept of scaling influence, I wrestle with how I'm primarily motivated by the results of my work as a connector. Am I being motivated by the value and meaning inherent in these relationships, or am I motivated by the profit that results from increased income opportunities or sales?

Sometimes the pursuit to grow or scale your influence may seem like a call to "more and more." At the same time, I think about stories of motivation that add meaning to scaling and collaboration. One example that comes to mind is in the *Lord of the Rings* trilogy by J. R. R. Tolkien, when Frodo and Sam are stranded on a mountain where an erupting volcano may soon end their quest. In that moment, they collapse, gasping for breath.

The dialogue then reads: "Do you remember the Shire, Mr. Frodo? It'll be spring soon. And the orchards will be in blossom. And the birds will be nesting in the hazel thicket. And they'll be sowing the summer barley in the lower fields ... and eating the first of the strawberries with cream. Do you remember the taste of strawberries?" (Tolkien, 1955).

Sam recalls the beauty of their homeland, and his little speech revives them to finish their quest—not knowing if they will ever see home again but keeping the beautiful memory of it as motivation for trying.

When you remember the benefit of helping others grow—the mutual joy of learning, the opportunity for new experiences, with or without the guarantee of reward—you will find your influence growing in beautiful ways. As a result of this kind of collaboration, you will be filling your barns (and the barns of others) with the right amount of produce for the days ahead.

Time for Reflection

1. What is something you are naturally good at doing that others may see as a superpower or wish they knew how to do?
2. When was the last time you asked someone to tell you their story and looked for the unique life lessons from that person?
3. In what ways could you serve more students, teachers, or leaders if you combined your skills and time with other educators like you?
4. What investments are you making in relationships so that, after people spend time with you, they feel like they have more ideas or motivation for what lies ahead?

CHAPTER 18

Pitching Yourself

The other day I was talking to a good friend who is an educator, a building-level leader as well as an author and presenter. He was lamenting how much he dislikes marketing or selling his books, content, and availability. This is fair and honest. Most of us cringe at the idea of someone pitching a product or service to us. Having said that, I'd like to challenge the notion of what it actually means to pitch yourself.

I'll begin by what I remember telling my friend: Most people spend most of their time thinking about themselves. I know that may seem a rude analysis of the human race, but let's face it. Most of us begin our days with questions like, "What will I eat and wear? What is my schedule? What people will I see today?" These questions prompt us to take care of ourselves so that we are ready to serve others.

Normally, these questions are followed by the ones where we think of others—usually, the people closest to us. "What are my loved ones doing? How can I help?" If you are a young parent, these questions are with you twenty-four hours a day.

I could be wrong, but I have found that most people are not asking who can help them accomplish the tasks or goals right in front of them. In other words, most people (short of those closest to you) are not thinking about you or how you can help them today. On the one hand, that is refreshing. On the other hand, if you have ideas, services, or solutions that can really help other people, it can be a maddening proposition to know how to offer those opportunities to others—especially if you are afraid of being perceived as pitching your professional services.

When you take the initiative to check in on others, share ways you can help, and offer them opportunities to connect, you are reminding them that you exist and may have something that can make their lives better. Here are some simple ways you can leverage your own professional growth, whether it is to expand the influence you have in your current role or whether you are looking for opportunities in other places:

1. *Share free lessons and content with others.*

As I've mentioned before, you are experienced in areas that could benefit someone else. As you are walking through a learning experience, write down a summary of what you're learning or record a short audio or video explaining those lessons. Keep it short and simple, and then share it with others through email, social media, or a direct contact. If you do this regularly, you can build a long list of your lessons or content that becomes a reservoir of information for your own reference and for others to learn from. You also build a reputation as someone who is adding value to the world based on your unique insights and perspective.

2. *Check in regularly with others.*

My friend Daniel Bauer, who has also served as a coach for me in business growth, shared a very practical tip. He said, "Will, if you check on ten to twenty people through a quick text or email just asking how they're doing and seeing if there is anything you can do to help—this kind of outreach alone will grow opportunities for you more than anything you do."

He is right, by the way. Since I made it a habit to check in on people, I have often found a moment like that turning into an invitation to talk on the phone, meet for a video chat, or come for a visit. A few weeks ago, I spoke to a small staff in a rural school district in western Oklahoma. Why? I had texted their superintendent to check in on him, and the exchange led to him asking me if I could present from my latest book to encourage his staff. Checking in may not seem like a way to pitch yourself, but it is relationship building that leads to the trust necessary for people to ask for help.

3. *Be a consultant, not a candidate.*

People do not hire you just to perform a service. People may need a service, but what they really need are meaningful solutions. Years ago, I decided to stop seeing interviews or meetings to consider my services as hiring opportunities. Instead, I ask myself, "What is an area of challenge where this person or group wants to be better? What questions can I ask that would help them consider new ideas or possible solutions?"

In other words, I began to see myself as a consultant with the ultimate goal of leaving people better than I found them. The result? I'm now spending my full-time work helping people. The vast majority of these opportunities came as a result of reaching out to others to see how I could help them reflect on challenges. The trust I built in those relationships has led to opportunities for ongoing collaboration and service.

When I was transitioning from assistant principal to head principal, I interviewed for four positions before I was offered the one where I finished my career as a high school principal. In one of those interviews, I remember thinking in advance, "I'm tired of trying to sell myself. Instead, I'm going to just explore ways I might help this team get better."

I went to the interview with an introduction, but I used the questions they asked me as ways to learn more about the school and offer suggestions on ways they may consider growth and solutions. After the interview, I received a polite call telling me they had chosen another candidate but appreciated my interview input. A while later, a friend of mine who worked for the district called. She explained that the team had already committed to another candidate, but after my interview, they debated what to do; because I had offered so many helpful suggestions, they were trying to decide how they could also hire me.

When you help others, they want to work with you—even if they cannot hire you in a traditional position. These opportunities build a reputation that often translates into other opportunities for you.

4. *Keep it simple and practical.*

As I said earlier, most people have not spent a lot of time thinking about you. When you have an opportunity to help others, make the most of the opportunity by introducing yourself with a summary of who you are and what you do. Sometimes I memorize an introduction. Mine sounds something like this:

> Hi, I'm Will Parker. I'm so grateful you gave me the opportunity to meet, as I know you have a lot of important responsibilities, and I may be only one of the people you're talking with today. I grew up in rural west Tennessee and never thought I'd go to college. I love learning, though, so I eventually moved to Oklahoma to attend college. I never thought I'd become an educator, but after finishing my degree, I decided to try teaching for a year or two.
>
> When I realized that being an educator was my calling, I spent twenty-four years as a teacher and school administrator before serving for six years as executive director of my state principals association. I'm an author, podcaster, and consultant, and I have done this work full time for Principal Matters, LLC, the past two years. I have a passion to help

others learn how to help themselves with innovative solutions that transform and improve the ways they serve their school communities.

This practical summary sets the stage for the ongoing conversation, and it helps others to hear the mission, vision, and practical ways your relationship may be mutually beneficial.

5. *Invite others to reflect together.*

Another productive way to pitch yourself is to invite others to reflect on their own journeys and challenges together. The beauty of these conversations is that you are inviting them to share their mission, vision, and challenges. Then you can use a series of reflection questions to explore what is on their mind, what they want to see happen, where you may be of help, and what strategies they may want to consider moving forward. These conversations can happen in fifteen minutes or sixty minutes. The key is to give someone else the freedom and trust to explore their own thinking in a safe space. This guided reflection time often leads to many *aha* moments and potential solutions neither of you had previously considered.

Let's Wrap This Up

In the case of my friend who was afraid of pitching herself, I reminded her that she has gifts, lessons, insights, and a unique perspective that can be a game changer for other educators in their own service to their school communities. Others deserve to be given the opportunity to benefit from her, and it is a kindness to let people know what you are learning and how it may help them in their own growth.

The same is true for you. Don't worry about the uncomfortable scenarios of "selling yourself" or the icky feeling of pitching yourself. Instead, be helpful:

- Invite others to share the areas where they want to see growth.
- Offer solutions or ideas when you can.
- Admit when you don't know the answers.
- Connect people with others who can help.

In the process, you are building a reputation as someone whose practices, experiences, and skills can help people.

Hopefully, these opportunities will also result in invitations to do new work with someone, and when they do, be prepared to share how much that time is worth to you and to them. Quantifying your time in terms of dollars and contracts is for another conversation, but making someone feel better than you found them is the best value you can exchange in any relationship. It is the best way to pitch yourself.

Time for Reflection

1. What is something you consider a fairly simple part of your job description? Who might benefit from learning this skill or insight from you and make it a game changer for their own practice?
2. Make a list of twenty people you consider colleagues or influencers in the work you love. Reach out to them with a short text or email. Ask them how they are doing and let them know you are cheering them on.
3. Based on responses to those emails, ask someone if they would like to connect for a conversation over coffee, by phone, or via Zoom to reflect on current challenges.
4. Rehearse an introduction that captures the mission and vision you have for doing the work you love. Practice saying this out loud, or video yourself saying it. Now change and edit that introduction for future use.

CHAPTER 19

Showcasing Your Profile

Several years ago, I was talking to a mentor leader, when he asked me to send him a copy of my professional vitae. I must admit, I said yes, but then I thought, "What is a professional vitae?"

A quick search showed me that a professional vitae, also called a *curriculum vitae*, is a fancy version of a résumé—with more of an emphasis on listing accomplishments, awards, presentations, and publications rather than just professional work history. I studied examples of what these models looked like for others, and I updated one for myself to match my real-life experiences in education. This practice reminded me of the ways I had been contributing to the growth of others in my own growth as an educator.

A few years later, I was talking to author Dr. Jen Schwanke about her great book *The Principal Reboot: 8 Ways to Revitalize Your School Leadership*. One of the suggestions she gives for leaders who need to rekindle some of the fire in their vision is to first sit down and update their résumé. The suggestion reminded me of what happened when I sent my updated work history through a professional vitae (Schwanke, 2020).

WHOSE PERMISSION ARE YOU WAITING FOR?

When you update your résumé, you give yourself permission to reflect on the historical perspective of the work you've done. You find reminders of ways you have done hard things in the past. You gain perspective on what is possible as you look toward the future. Because I have been asked so often to share a copy of my résumé, I am going to include an example from a few years ago to show how I've showcased my own experience. I always keep in mind that it represents just a glimpse of thirty years of work:

Résumé Sample

William D. Parker
Owasso, Oklahoma
Email: will@williamdparker.com
Website: www.williamdparker.com

Skills
- 30 years of experience as an educator in roles as teacher, administrator, executive director, and education consultant.
- Proven skills in instructing and motivating others.
- Responsible for creating and maintaining strategic plans and facilitating professional learning.
- Knowledgeable in managing contracts, administering budgets, leading staff development, and hiring and supervising others.
- Described as a take-charge, creative, diplomatic person.

Leadership
- Author, consultant, blogger, podcaster, and keynote speaker.
- Certified as a teacher, principal, and superintendent.
- Experienced in executive coaching, organizing workshops, and conferences for in-person or hybrid settings.

- Skilled in communicating with others in person, in writing, or across multiple media platforms to establish rapport and support.
- Experienced in public relations and successful in handling negotiations with multiple parties to achieve collaborative solutions.

Qualifications
- Founder of Principal Matters, LLC, serving educators globally.
- Led a 501(c)(6) association with 3,000 members, coordinating services, training, support, and conferences. Directly supported 900 secondary principals.
- Increased membership by over 10% in five years.
- As a former principal and assistant principal, managed schools with student populations of 700 to 1,300 in the Tulsa, Oklahoma area.
- Created and supervised innovative programs to enhance school success.
- Able to work independently and collaboratively.

Professional Growth
- Extensive experience in instruction and program development.
- Presenter or keynote speaker on school leadership topics at over 120 live or virtual events in 15 states across the United States, including Washington, D.C., for public, private, and charter school educators.
- Confident in small- and large-group settings.
- Works well with all levels of leadership.
- Author of three books and content creator of over 350 podcast episodes with more than 1 million downloads.
- Awarded South Intermediate High School Teacher of the Year (1998) and Oklahoma Assistant Principal of the Year (2012).

Experience
PRESENT
Principal Matters, LLC – Tulsa, Oklahoma
Author, Speaker, Education Consultant

July 2017–June 2023
Cooperative Council of School Administrators – Oklahoma City, Oklahoma
Executive Director, Oklahoma Association of Secondary Principals and Oklahoma Middle Level Education Association

2012–2017
Skiatook Public Schools – Skiatook, Oklahoma
High School Principal

2006–2012
Skiatook Public Schools – Skiatook, Oklahoma
High School Assistant Principal

2004–2006
Bixby Public Schools – Bixby, Oklahoma
High School Assistant Principal

2001–2004
Catoosa Public Schools – Catoosa, Oklahoma
Advanced Placement English Teacher, Department Chair

1993–2001
Broken Arrow Public Schools – Broken Arrow, Oklahoma
South Intermediate High School, Language Arts Teacher

Contact
References available upon request.

A Few Résumé Pointers

Headings and short descriptions capture a running testimony of work done over the decades. If you're just beginning your professional journey, remember to include the steps that led you to where you are today—including outside the profession.

For seasoned educators, you must decide what not to include. If you try to include all your assignments or committees, for instance, you may overwhelm someone reviewing your history.

Letters of Endorsement

If you've never asked for a letter of recommendation, ask trusted colleagues, leaders, or former coworkers if they could write a letter explaining why they would recommend you for whatever position you're considering or pursuing.

Whenever I consult, present, or coach, I usually reach out to the client who hired me and ask them for a letter of endorsement or even just a short paragraph. I include these on my website and in the prospective documents I send to clients. If you'd like to see a copy of mine, you can visit my website at williamdparker.com/endorsements. Here are three examples:

> "William's words were powerful, and his advice of telling your story on social media changed a community's perception of a school that had been impacted by trauma and negativity for many years. The continued impact endures in students, staff, families, and community members. As a leader, I have never been directly impacted by such transformational change which occurred through stories. William continues to impact Dimmitt Middle School, and we are thankful for the stories he shared with all the Renton School District leaders."
> —Gioia Pitts, Chief of Secondary Schools, Renton School District, Greater Seattle Area, Washington

"Will's approach engages each leader in the development of critical leadership skills. Using guided reflections, book studies, sharing best practices, and the principles contained in his books, his sessions allow leaders to reflect and improve their approach to leadership and engaging staff, students, and the community. Our school leaders look forward to each meeting and have requested that we continue to offer Will's program."
—Shelia P. Vitale, Esq. Director Office of Ohio School Sponsorship

"Will Parker was the highlight of our conference. His keynote and breakout sessions provided our group with professional development that could not have been more poignant. He spoke to the teachers about the message of their classroom and how they communicate with their students. He then flipped right around and spoke to a standing-room-only group of administrators about the hats they must wear to be a successful leader. I can't tell you the number of people who approached me to thank me for bringing Will Parker to the conference. If you would like a brilliant, approachable, and engaging speaker for your next PD, there is only one choice . . . Will Parker."
—Tomas Mascaluso, President, Nevada Association of Career and Technical Education

These statements help build your credibility with future audiences as well as remind you of the value you have provided in past settings. A quick email or text to a decision maker in those settings is the best way to ask for this kind of feedback.

A Website or Webpage

Whether you created your own Google page or purchased a web address, having your own website or webpage is a great way to showcase your profile, including examples of your work and highlights from your experience. In a world of constantly changing social media channels and options, a webpage is a way for you to own your own space online without someone else deciding how to platform it for you. If you're interested in a free option, try Google Sites, WordPress, or Wix.

When I began my website by using a self-hosted WordPress option, I relied on a tutorial available from Michael Hyatt on how to begin using it (Hyatt, 2016). Google Sites has its own support page to get you started (Google, 2024). You could also hire someone on a part-time basis to build one for you. For instance, Lisa Parry, a friend and fellow educator, has a beautiful website her daughter helped her build that highlights her work as an educator, teacher, principal, and motivational speaker. You can see it at https://www.principalparry.com/.

Whatever platform you choose, it is important to include a way for people to contact you when they visit your page. I also integrate my website with Mailchimp, a platform that allows others to subscribe for receiving updates from me. You can find other email services that integrate with a website by checking out ConstantContact.com, Mailchimp.com, or Hubspot.com.

LinkedIn or other Social Media

Even with all the social media options available, I have found LinkedIn one of the most consistent places for profiling professional credentials and following others with similar interests. I also use X (previously Twitter) as well as Facebook, Instagram, and Threads. I know many educators who also successfully use YouTube and TikTok. Whatever platform you use, the key is that duplication is OK. Whatever you post on one platform can be quickly edited and posted on another. Because each platform has a uniquely different audience, social media opens up opportunities to connect with and meet people you may not know otherwise.

Promo Video

This may not be an option that resonates with everyone, but when you're trying to introduce yourself or your work to others in a captivating way, consider creating a promotional video. In 2015, I paid a videographer to follow me around for a few hours, and he created a two-minute promotional video highlighting the work I was doing with educators and students. It also served as a way to introduce my first book. Because it is dated, I no longer use it, but it opened many doors for me in my initial years of building a network for speaking.

If you want to create your own promotional video, use your own personal device, like your phone, tablet, or webcam, to record a quick greeting for people interested in seeing you in action before reaching out to you for a conversation.

Let's Wrap This Up

Whatever options you choose for an online presence, remember that digital copy becomes dated very quickly. By the time this goes to print, it is possible many of the tips I just gave you have been preempted by other technologies, including AI options, that you could also keep in mind.

Even with the risk of digital portfolios becoming quickly outdated, the practice of cataloging your history of work through your résumé, website, endorsements, social media channels, or promotional videos are all helpful ways to grow your professional network. Most importantly, building relationships with others always trumps any digital footprint you may have. At the same time, a digital portfolio may open doors for new relationships.

Time for Reflection

1. What online platforms are you currently using for your work history and professional offerings?
2. When was the last time you updated your résumé? Consider having someone look it over to see if they have suggestions for improvement.
3. Consistency is one of the best policies for updating websites and social media platforms. Could you post something on your platforms at least once a week? Pick a weekly day and time and commit to posting for one year to see what happens.

CHAPTER 20

Applying Cycles for All of Life

A few mornings ago at the time of this writing, I went for a jog with my dog Ivy. As I walked the stretch of road to cool down on the way back to my front door, I was thinking about this book. "Who is going to want to read a book about permission to do what you love?" I thought to myself.

Most books for educators cover topics about teaching practice, classroom management, having hard conversations, or even educator self-care. My other books have ranged in topics from leadership tips for new principals to communication tips for school messaging. And I wanted to write a book on lessons for educators trying to navigate the tricky roads of professional pathways, hard decisions, or next steps in a career? Really?

Later that morning, I logged into a Zoom call I had scheduled with a listener to my podcast. I meet a lot of educators this way. Someone will hear something that is helpful in an episode, and I may receive an email asking for a resource I've mentioned. I'm intrigued about their education journey, and we will schedule a call to learn more about each other's work. In this case, I was talking to a young administrator in her second year as a campus principal—in a relatively small Christian school not far from Chicago.

I asked her what was on her mind, and she told me about the goals her school had in the year ahead. We talked about ways to maximize her digital footprint. Then she asked me, "I'm curious about what I can be doing as I think about the years ahead. My own children attend a school in my neighborhood where I'd love them to stay, and it's possible they will have an opening for an administrator there. How do I know when it's time to begin conversations about what's next? When should I bring my own supervisor into my thoughts about a transition? When is it appropriate to reach out to someone with whom you're interested in working next?"

I had to pause and think, "Well, there is at least one person out there who may benefit from this book!"

The truth of the matter is there are many, many people with whom I have had this conversation. This school year alone, I have already scheduled more than one hundred one-on-one coaching conversations. Many of them will be about solving challenges specific to each of their schools, districts, or systems. At the same time, most of these leaders at some point will ask me a question connected to the topics we have covered in this book. It is for them, and hopefully for you, that I've written this book.

Having said that, I'd like to wrap up this long conversation—this walk through problem solving, network building, Odyssey planning, and so much more with one simple observation:

The cycles of learning you have practiced that brought you to the place where you are today will likely be the cycles of learning you will practice to take you to where you are going next.

Good teaching involves the ability to first disrupt the thinking of a learner. In other words, a person is not ready for new thinking unless you can somehow challenge their current thinking. When we become

APPLYING CYCLES FOR ALL OF LIFE

aware of our need to understand new information, then we are prepared to tackle a new idea.

With new information comes the need to apply that knowledge. When you apply the knowledge, you then must access what worked and what did not work. Then you move forward armed with experience, and the cycle repeats itself again.

> Good teaching involves the ability to first disrupt the thinking of a learner.

As an educator, you are a leader of learning. If you ever stop applying those same reflective cycles to your own learning, then you will no longer be able to lead others in their own growth. Stop growing, and you actually begin declining. No one is allowed to coast if they want to experience gains in knowledge and experience.

Recently, I heard a guest on the Ted Radio Hour Podcast. Jennifer Vail (2022), a tribologist (someone who specializes in the science of friction), explained how we need friction and the right amount of stress to keep us motivated. We need friction for rubber tires to carry our cars along roadways, for electricity to pulse through systems, and for us to build stronger muscles and endurance.

Friction can be a good thing. Too much of it can cause machines and people to break. Just the right amount can cause others to hum along. As you think about the pathway in front of you, I want to remind you of the importance of reflection for your own pathways, inquiry as a tool for relationships, and future planning that influences all of life.

> Friction can be a good thing. Too much of it can cause machines and people to break. Just the right amount can cause others to hum along.

WHOSE PERMISSION ARE YOU WAITING FOR?

Think back to lessons we've covered together, and ask yourself what lessons you have learned and what lessons you are learning. Beside each statement, write a number between 1 and 5 to show whether you would mark this as a low commitment (1 or 2), a moderate commitment (3), or a high commitment (4 or 5):

- I recognize that fixed-mindset pathways are limiting, and I commit to exploring growth-mindset models, which offer multiple routes if I am willing to explore them.
- I will avoid binary thinking and explore different pathways and opportunities, as shown through Odyssey plans.
- I commit to nurturing my curiosity through inquiry, knowing it will lead to new discoveries. I will use tools such as interviewing others, onsite exploration, podcasts, books, biographies, and note-taking.
- I understand that effective decision making requires me to grasp complexity, which will eventually lead to simplicity.
- I will stay consistent in my growth, knowing that small actions build momentum. I commit to mastering my skills through years of practice and dedication.
- I embrace the concept of "Will it fly?" by testing my ideas through beta testing and real-world application. I will build something when I see a need, rather than imagining one that doesn't exist.
- I will stop waiting for permission to explore my areas of curiosity and inquiry—I will act now and create my own opportunities.
- I commit to seeing my skills rewarded by identifying opportunities for growth within salaried positions, gig work, or ownership.
- I recognize the importance of building systems and strategies, including calendars, tools, and tax planning, especially as I explore managing myself.

APPLYING CYCLES FOR ALL OF LIFE

- I will consistently reflect on my life, set monthly and weekly goals, and assess daily tasks to maintain focus.
- I see the value in coaching and will engage in both receiving guidance and offering it to others.
- I will join groups of like-minded leaders to support continuous learning, reflection, and problem solving within a community.
- I understand that rituals and habits (e.g., sleep, nutrition, movement, etc.) shape my life and contribute to my productivity and well-being. I will find joy in my work and pay attention to where I find motivation and moments of personal realization.
- I will seek mentorship to pass on knowledge to others, avoiding the tendency to become an "advice monster."
- I will imagine my goals exponentially bigger, expanding my possibilities and pushing beyond a scarcity mindset.
- I will use backward mapping to plan forward, starting with a clear destination and working in reverse.
- I will focus on scaling my influence by lifting others up, networking, and leaving a positive impact wherever I go.
- I commit to sharing my value with others, even if it feels uncomfortable. I will learn to highlight my strengths and make connections.
- I will regularly update my profile, résumé, and accomplishments to reflect my growth and successes.
- I will embrace life's cycles of reflection, inquiry, and planning apply to all areas of my life, including relationships, career, and personal growth.

Now add up the total numbers. Out of a possible one hundred points, what is your commitment to the practices we have covered that may help you stop waiting for permission to do what you love?

If you've read this far, I want to commend you for being a student of what works for others and then applying those lessons to yourself.

Most importantly, choose one idea or thought you can take action on today. None of us ever perfects the actions involved in these cycles, but small, consistent efforts over time can make an enormous difference.

Let's Wrap This Up

One of my podcast guests, Carlos Johnson, author of *Power Engage: Seven Power Moves for Building Strong Relationships to Increase Engagement with Students and Parents*, shared some research that has motivated him toward small, consistent action. He explains the Domino-Effect Model, created by Professor Stepen Morris from Toronto University.

The professor creates a model of thirteen dominos, the smallest of which is five millimeters tall–the size of a pencil eraser. Each domino in procession is 1.5 times larger than the one before. The thirteenth domino is about three feet tall and weighs more than one hundred pounds. He shows how the falling of the first tiny domino creates enough force to knock down the largest. He then explains that if he continued to twenty-nine dominoes, the last domino would be the size of the Empire State Building (Johnson, 2024).

Obviously, the mathematical and scientific implications of matter working on matter are not directly correlated to the dynamics involved in human behavior, relationships, or actions. At the same time, we can apply the lesson to our understanding of our own actions.

What happens when you take small actions over time that build on the collective knowledge, understanding, and momentum involved in personal growth and learning? You may not see the impact as clearly as a domino the size of a skyscraper, but you can see it in the impact others have had in shaping what you have become.

Each of us is the product of the people who have invested in us. Our parents, teachers, mentors, coaches, pastors, authors, movie makers, musicians, politicians, neighbors, and lovers—all of these have played a small or big part in the motion of our lives. We really do stand on the shoulders of others when we look around at the place where we've landed in life.

Time for Reflection

1. Of the lessons listed in this chapter, which one has been most helpful to you in reading this book, and why?
2. What is one action you have taken as a result of reflecting on the cycles of learning?
3. What is one action you plan to take today to keep the momentum going as you continue your personal and professional growth?

CONCLUSION

A Final Conversation Walking Together

When I was five years old, my family moved to west Tennessee from San Diego, California. My father had completed a long career in the Navy, and he decided it was time to move his wife and five children back home. During his years in the Navy, my dad had bought 120 acres adjacent to the farmland my grandfather and his family owned.

Large oak and walnut trees surrounded the remains of an old farmhouse that had burned down years before. This would become the spot where my dad and his brother would dig a 50×30-foot hole for a basement lined with cinderblock walls. The home had a single entry with ground-level side windows and a chimney in the middle of the structure, and it was covered with a flat roof. Someday, a two-story home would be built on the structure, but for six years, that basement would become our home.

The same day we visited the property for the first time, my dad took all five children for a walk across the land. A forty-acre field carved out the northern point of the farm, which touched the gravel road that divided our land from my grandfather's. The southern half of the farm was another eighty acres of field that could be used for crops or grazing pasture. The rest of the land was woods, creeks, and gullies.

We walked with my dad to the farthest end and through some wooded areas where an old field road lined its way through a tunnel of trees. We stepped out of this enclosure into knee-high sagebrush. Woods of pines and oaks walled us in from both sides of the large pasture. I was only five years old, and my goal was to keep up with my dad, my three older brothers, and my younger sister.

Suddenly, my dad stopped.

"Listen," he said. "We've walked a long way from the road, and I've been leading the whole way. I'd like you all to find our way back without my help."

We looked at each other, puzzled and curious.

"Well," said my oldest brother, Harvey. "I think we came from that way." He pointed in the direction he thought we should go.

"Are you sure?" asked my second brother, Jesse. "I think we're supposed to look at the sun and figure out which way to go."

The arguing continued until one of us suggested we walk in the field until we saw something familiar. So, we walked. My dad kept his place behind us so that we were forced to discuss our progress and choose our way forward without his help. Before long, we came to a bend in the field, and ahead of us, we could see where the field led to a familiar space. Not long afterward, we found the old homeplace.

It is one of my first memories there, and I still remember the sense of relief and joy in knowing we had found our way home—even though we hadn't yet built the one we would live in.

I think a lot of my life has been inspired by moments like that walk in the field. Because my father never earned much money in part-time farming, he also worked as an electrician and later started his own marine salvage business. Whatever his work, he was always interested in learning.

A FINAL CONVERSATION WALKING TOGETHER

For years, he owned beehives, and he taught us how to retrieve golden honey and combs we would jar and enjoy all year long. We kept two milk cows that had been tended morning and night, and we enjoyed the rich, creamy milk and butter they produced. I dug potatoes with my father and remembered the joy of those fresh, soft, red-skinned steamy wonders as we ate them for dinner. We fetched water from a spring until my dad dug a well and plumbed the basement home. At the time, I didn't realize how often my father created learning moments.

I remember the quiet evenings when the five of us would gather around my dad and he would open a book of fairy tales and read to us before we fell asleep. Dad never finished high school, but he had earned a GED while serving in the Navy, and he and my mother did their best to surround us with as many books as they could. Storytelling was also an important tradition in our family. It was how we held on to memories.

I love adventure, and although my path has taken me away to another state and sometimes around the world, I still enjoy returning home to west Tennessee each year. My own four children, three of them adults and one in high school, consider Christmas time in Tennessee a sacred tradition that I'm grateful we can all still enjoy.

After I found my footing as a young teacher, I saw the classroom as a place where students should not only encounter content standards but also have memorable learning experiences. For instance, one day I brought bags of found objects to class. Students closed their eyes while I placed items on their desks. They each had one minute to feel the objects, poke and prod them, smell them, and lift them. Then I collected the objects. For the next ten minutes, they wrote—describing in as much detail as possible the intricacies of the thing they held.

Then they took turns reading their descriptions aloud, allowing the others to guess what the object was, its color, or its dimensions before I would pull it from the bag to compare it to the student's description.

WHOSE PERMISSION ARE YOU WAITING FOR?

Yes, the state learning standards for 9th grade language arts included composing a strong paragraph structure using various literary forms, including descriptive, expository, and argumentative writing. However, I was discovering that their words created imagery, sparked imagination, and could even inspire joy and curiosity.

In 2012, when I was named Oklahoma Assistant Principal of the Year by the National Association of Secondary School Principals and invited to a ceremony in Washington, D.C., I was so inspired by a room full of fellow education leaders from almost every state who were also being recognized. It was the first time in my education career that my perspective was suddenly so much bigger than my own school, my own community, or my own state. I realized that I was part of a community of other educators who were experiencing similar challenges, joys, griefs, and lessons so much like my own—and yet so different from my own as well.

After that trip, I felt compelled to begin telling my own stories in education. I researched how to start a website, and in February 2013, I created my very first blog post. Each week, I would write about something I was learning, and I would post it.

At the same time I was stepping into my years as a high school principal, my writing was leading to invitations to present or speak at conferences for education leaders. I was publishing a book with Solution Tree Press when our state principal association reached out with an invitation to apply for an executive director opening. I said yes, and my twenty-four years of serving in schools then pivoted for the next five years to serving school leaders.

In 2020, I wrote my third book *Pause. Breathe. Flourish. Living Your Best Life as an Educator* with ConnectEDD Publishing. Soon after, I launched my first mastermind offerings for weekly virtual meetings of leaders from across the United States. This book is coming out at the end of my second year in the adventure of full-time consulting, and frankly, it has worked out better than anticipated.

A FINAL CONVERSATION WALKING TOGETHER

Why the personal history throughout this book? I have discovered most of our stories have a lot in common. We each have a personal journey that is tailored to our unique gifts and talents. We each make decisions along the way that either keep us motivated or weigh us down with doubts. We each bring a perspective or experience that belongs only to us. And each of us is part of something bigger than we are.

> We each have a personal journey that is tailored to our unique gifts and talents.

The cycles of learning I share in this book are also the ones I have been practicing and learning in my own journey and pathway. As you look at your own journey, I'm curious if you are reflecting on where your adventure is taking you. Are you still waiting for someone's permission to do what you love? If so, let me encourage you to consider the following questions:

1. *Where have you been, and where are you going?*

Take an inventory of your journey. Making a list of milestones you have reached can provide perspective on the hard work it has taken for you to reach this point in your life and career.

One practical way to do this is by updating your résumé. Another may be to make a chronological record of the past three to five years of goals you have set and reached. As you reflect on where you have been, then the question becomes "Where I am going next?" Each day, week, month, and year—you have the opportunity to set goals for new ideas, opportunities, and experiences.

Another way I do this is by taking an inventory of my life, including both personal and professional. This inventory then helps me set new goals for growth in personal health, relationship development, and career goals.

2. *How do you use the wisdom of others and lessons learned to give you insights for tomorrow?*

The complexities we face in working with others require more than a prescriptive formula. By studying the lives of others who have found solutions, success, or meaning in their work, we can glean ideas from them that may help us apply the same truths to our own context. Reading biographies, interviewing people you find inspiring, or spending time with mentors you admire—all of these sources allow us to reflect on our experiences in our own journeys.

3. *How are you expressing gratitude for those with whom you are learning, for those with whom you can share the journey, or for those with whom you can tell your stories?*

Who has helped you grow, provided you with resources, and supported the work you do? Take time to tell them thank you. Gratitude helps us walk humbly, knowing that none of us is truly independent. If we are accomplishing great things, it is directly connected to ways others are supporting us and helping make our work possible.

Let's Wrap This Up

One day in high school, I was hiking in the fields and woods behind my childhood home. It was a wintry afternoon when I set out, and I was wearing plenty of layers, including gloves and a knitted hat. The woods and gullies near our house were filled with oaks, holly trees, and evergreens. Thick blankets of leaves and pine needles covered the grounds there. Farther along the creek bed, you could find a beaver dam. And if you sat long enough on the water's bank, you may have seen a gray egret or a flock of ducks land in front of you to forage for food.

I worked my way through the woods and up a fence line until I stepped out into an open field—the same one my father had led us into my first time on the farm when I was five years old. The sun was setting in the west, but I couldn't see it, because the clouds were thick overhead and dusk was quickly turning to dark.

I kept moving north in the direction of the house, but a few minutes later, the darkness deepened. Suddenly, I realized I couldn't see but a few feet in front of me. Thankfully, I was intimately familiar with my surroundings, but, at the same time, it is not easy to find your way in darkness. I could tell that I was still in the field where I had started heading north, but I was having difficulty knowing exactly how far it would be before I'd reach home. The temperature began to drop, and I was feeling the cold closing in.

I didn't panic, but thoughts began pressing into my mind as I walked. What if I go in the wrong direction and I don't know it? What happens if I get turned around and find myself freezing and lost? This was also before anyone carried smartphones. At this point, I said a prayer and hoped I could also depend on my sense of direction.

Slowly, I kept plodding ahead, my boots pushing through dry sagebrush. My eyes scanned for any sign that I was on the right path. Just then, I saw a faint light flicker to my right. I walked a few steps more and saw a warm, orange light.

I stood still, trying to make sense of this small, bright orb, when I realized it was a single window. It took me a few seconds to realize it was a window in my house across the field. The entire structure was swallowed by darkness, but the single, orange window shone like the beacon of a welcome friend. It's hard to describe the feeling I had at that moment. I had looked at my home thousands of times. I could describe the angles of the roof and the placement of every door and window. But I had never known how beautiful the light of a single window could look when you're feeling cold and lost.

At times when I'm traveling far from home, speaking in an unfamiliar city, or driving the roads of a town or state I've never visited before, I'll imagine the light of that window. The warmth of home promises a safe place where you find your food, rest, and kin. It is a place where you share stories of your adventures. It is a promised refuge even in moments of unexpected darkness. Sometimes we have the comfort of knowing we are heading in the right direction after all.

Perhaps you're trying to solve some difficult challenges in your own responsibilities as an educator. Maybe you are attempting to navigate the next choices in your position or career. It's possible you have a friend, team member, or student to whom you are responsible for coaching, mentoring, or advice. I believe each of us finds the path of decision making a little easier to navigate when we take time to reflect and apply the lessons we've learned together along the way. Will you give yourself permission to stay adventurous?

Thank you for joining me on a journey—a cycle of lessons that may help you in your reflection, focus, and action in your own learning and life adventures. As you continue walking your pathway in education and life, please savor the moments you're in, trust your sense of direction, and say a prayer for what is and what is not in your control.

In the meantime, learning from one another is a good way to not lose your direction. As someone goes ahead of us, we can look at the light that shines back in our direction and find our way with a little more clarity.

Perhaps this book has been a small light to help you along your path. If I'm able to help you with more feedback, a conversation, or just taking a walk together, please let me know. Either way, I'll keep a light on for you in case you decide to look me up.

References

Albinia, Alice. *The Britannias: An Archipelago's Tale*. W. W. Norton, 2024.

Allegretto, Sylvia. "Teacher Pay Penalty Still Looms Large: Trends in Teacher Wages and Compensation Through 2022." *Economic Policy Institute*, September 29, 2023. https://www.epi.org/publication/teacher-pay-in-2022/.

Bauer, Daniel. Mastermind: *Unlocking Talent Within Every School Leader*. Corwin, AASA, 2022a.

Bauer, Daniel. "Meet Daniel." Better Leaders Better Schools, 2022b, https://betterleadersbetterschools.com/meet-daniel/.

Boey, Matthew. "Learning from the Best: Singapore and Education Reform." *The Public Purpose*, September 18, 2019. https://thepublicpurpose.com/2019/09/18/learning-from-the-best-singapore-and-education-reform/.

Bungay Stanier, Michael. *The Advice Trap: Be Humble, Stay Curious and Change the Way You Lead Forever*. Box of Crayons Press, 2020.

Burnett, Bill, and Dave Evans. *Designing Your Life: How to Build a Well-Lived, Joyful Life*. Alfred A. Knopf, 2016.

Chester, John, dir. *The Biggest Little Farm*. FarmLore Films, Neon, 2018.

Clear, James. *Atomic Habits: An Easy & Proven Way to Build Good Habits and Break Bad Ones*. Avery, 2018.

"#DeepThought Classroom Discussion." YouTube, uploaded by PedaLOGICAL- Logically Thinking About Teaching, January 4, 2017, https://www.youtube.com/watch?v=C9t6g6wtpBY.

Flynn, Pat. "SPI 778: Inside a Pat Flynn Coaching Call with Cassie Shawcross." YouTube, uploaded by Smart Passive Income, April 19, 2024, https://www.youtube.com/watch?v=GDZLh5CySRY.

Flynn, Pat. "How to Start a Podcast Tutorial." Smart Passive Income, 2023, https://www.smartpassiveincome.com/guides/how-to-start-a-podcast-tutorial-pat-flynn/.

Flynn, Pat. "How to Start a Podcast." YouTube, uploaded by Pat Flynn, December 14, 2021, https://www.youtube.com/watch?v=Q8pfZna6H6Q.

Flynn, Pat. *Will It Fly? How to Test Your Next Business Idea So You Don't Waste Your Time and Money*. Flynndustries, LLC, 2016.

Full Focus. LifeScore Assessment, 2024, https://assessments.fullfocus.co/lifescore/.

Gladwell, Malcolm. *Outliers: The Story of Success*. Little, Brown and Company, 2011.

Google. "Create, name, or copy a site." *Google Support*, Google, 2024, https://support.google.com/sites/answer/98081?hl=en.

Hall, Pete, and Alisa Simeral. *Teach, Reflect, Learn: Building Your Capacity for Success in the Classroom*. ASCD, 2015.

Horn, Sam. *Someday Is Not a Day in the Week: 10 Hacks to Make the Rest of Your Life the Best of Your Life*. St. Martin's Press, 2019.

Hyatt, Michael. "How to Set Up a Self-Hosted WordPress Blog in 20 Minutes or Less." *YouTube*, 2016, https://www.youtube.com/watch?v=OFLk3srgg1M.

Hyatt, Michael. "How to Start a Blog in 4 Easy Steps." YouTube, uploaded by Michael Hyatt, July 13, 2013, https://www.youtube.com/watch?v=8jJ8v17CgPo&t=5.

Hyatt, Michael. *Platform: Get Noticed in a Noisy World*. Thomas Nelson, 2012.

Johnson, Carlos. *Power Engage: Seven Power Moves for Building Strong Relationships to Increase Engagement with Students and Parents*. Solution Tree Press, 2024.

Kawasaki, Guy, and Madisun Nuismer. *Think Remarkable: 9 Paths to Transform Your Life and Make a Difference*. Wiley, 2024, 175–176.

Kubicek, Jeremie, and Steve Cochran. *The 5 Voices: How to Communicate Effectively with Everyone You Lead*. Wiley, 2016.

REFERENCES

Lencioni, Patrick M. *The 6 Types of Working Genius: A Better Way to Understand Your Gifts, Your Frustrations, and Your Team.* The Table Group, 2022.

McCullough, David. *The Wright Brothers.* Simon & Schuster, 2015.

National SAM Innovation Project. "Research on SAM Process." NSIP, 2022, https://www.nationalsams.com/copy-of-research.

National Institutes of Health. "Sleep Deprivation Increases Alzheimer's Protein." NIH Research Matters, April, 24, 2018, www.nih.gov/news-events/nih-research-matters/sleep-deprivation-increases-alzheimers-protein.

Nyad, Diana. "Never, Ever Give Up." TED, December 2013, www.ted.com.

Oklahoma State University. "Project ECHO." Oklahoma State University Center for Health Sciences, 2024, https://medicine.okstate.edu/echo/.

Parker, William. "PMP426: What Makes a Great Principal with George Couros." *Principal Matters* [podcast], December 11, 2024a, https://www.williamdparker.com.

Parker, William. "PMP414: Managing Your Priorities with Mark Shellinger." *Principal Matters* [podcast], October 9, 2024b, https://williamdparker.com/2024/pmp414-managing-your-priorities-with-mark-shellinger/.

Parker, William D. "PMP366: Navigating Leadership Drift." *Principal Matters* [podcast], October 18, 2023, https://williamdparker.com/2023/pmp366-navigating-leadership-drift-with-cale-birk/.

Parker, William D. "PMP169: Leading into the Wind – Lessons from Dave Sandowich." *Principal Matters* [podcast], October 23, 2019, https://williamdparker.com/2019/pmp169-leading-into-the-wind-lessons-from-dave-sandowich/.

Pink, Daniel H. *The Power of Regret: How Looking Backward Moves Us Forward.* Riverhead Books, 2022.

Ramsey, Dave. *EntreLeadership: 20 Years of Practical Business Wisdom from the Trenches.* Howard Books, 2011.

Schnall, Simone, Kent D. Harber, Jeanine K. Stefanucci, and Dennis R. Proffitt. "Social Support and the Perception of Geographical Slant." *Journal of Experimental Social Psychology,* 44(5), 2008: 1246–1255.

Schwanke, Jen. *The Principal Reboot: 8 Ways to Revitalize Your School Leadership.* ASCD, 2020.

Skillicorn, Nick. "The 10,000-Hour Rule Was Wrong, According to the People Who Wrote the Original Study: What Is Really Required to Become an Expert Is Very Different." Idea to Value, June 9, 2016, www.ideatovalue.com.

Stanier, Michael Bungay. *The Coaching Habit: Say Less, Ask More and Change the Way You Lead Forever*. Box of Crayons Press, 2016.

Sullivan, Dan, and Benjamin Hardy. *10x Is Easier Than 2x: How World-Class Entrepreneurs Achieve More by Doing Less*. Hay House, 2023.

Tolkien, J. R. R. *The Return of the King*. George Allen & Unwin, 1955.

Vail, Jennifer. Ted Radio Hour. NPR, September 30, 2022, https://www.npr.org/programs/ted-radio-hour/1127240880/friction.

Vendantum, Shankar. "You 2.0: The Gift of Other People." *Hidden Brain* [podcast], July 31, 2023, https://hiddenbrain.org/podcast/you-2-0-the-gift-of-other-people/.

Williamson, Marianne. *A Return to Love: Reflections on the Principles of "A Course in Miracles."* HarperCollins, 1992.

Zomorodi, Manoush, host. "Introducing Body Electric." TED Radio Hour, NPR, November 14, 2023, www.npr.org/2023/11/14/1213000342/introducing-body-electric-with-manoush-zomorodi.

Acknowledgements

I want to thank Megan Doyle, from Alexandria, Virginia, who assisted me in proofing my original manuscript. Also, gratitude to Jimmy Casas, for inspiring me and inviting me to another publication with ConnectEDD Publishing. The talents of Jeff Zoul provided both editorial precision and thoughtful feedback–thank you, Jeff, for your invaluable wisdom and guidance! To the many educators who have trusted me as a coach, consultant, and confidant: Your questions and honest conversations gave me the real-life material for which to write this book. A special thanks to the Spears family for the use of their farmhouse for writing and editing. Finally, I want to thank my wife, Missy, and our children Emily, Mattie, Katie, and Jack, for encouraging me to do work I love.

About the Author

William D. Parker is the founder of Principal Matters, LLC, an educator, author, speaker, and executive coach who uses his expertise in school culture, leadership, and communication to equip educators with solutions and strategies for motivating students, inspiring teachers, and reaching communities.

Will serves schools across the globe through professional development and leadership support. He is regularly asked to present at K–12 professional development events, education conferences, leadership teams, and graduate classes on effective practices, organizational management, and strategies for enhancing school communication. Find out more or book him to present at www.williamdparker.com.

More from ConnectEDD Publishing

Since 2015, ConnectEDD has worked to transform education by empowering educators to become better-equipped to teach, learn, and lead. What started as a small company designed to provide professional learning events for educators has grown to include a variety of services to help educators and administrators address essential challenges. ConnectEDD offers instructional and leadership coaching, professional development workshops focusing on a variety of educational topics, a roster of nationally recognized educator associates who possess hands-on knowledge and experience, educational conferences custom-designed to meet the specific needs of schools, districts, and state/national organizations, and ongoing, personalized support, both virtually and onsite. In 2020, ConnectEDD expanded to include publishing services designed to provide busy educators with books and resources consisting of practical information on a wide variety of teaching, learning, and leadership topics. Please visit us online at connecteddpublishing.com or contact us at: info@connecteddpublishing.com

Recent Publications:

Live Your Excellence: Action Guide by Jimmy Casas

Culturize: Action Guide by Jimmy Casas

Daily Inspiration for Educators: Positive Thoughts for Every Day of the Year by Jimmy Casas

Eyes on Culture: Multiply Excellence in Your School by Emily Paschall

Pause. Breathe. Flourish. Living Your Best Life as an Educator by William D. Parker

L.E.A.R.N.E.R. Finding the True, Good, and Beautiful in Education by Marita Diffenbaugh

Educator Reflection Tips Volume II: Refining Our Practice by Jami Fowler-White

Handle With Care: Managing Difficult Situations in Schools with Dignity and Respect by Jimmy Casas and Joy Kelly

Disruptive Thinking: Preparing Learners for Their Future by Eric Sheninger

Permission to be Great: Increasing Engagement in Your School by Dan Butler

Daily Inspiration for Educators: Positive Thoughts for Every Day of the Year, Volume II by Jimmy Casas

The 6 Literacy Levers: Creating a Community of Readers by Brad Gustafson

The Educator's ATLAS: Your Roadmap to Engagement by Weston Kieschnick

MORE FROM CONNECTEDD PUBLISHING

In This Season: Words for the Heart by Todd Nesloney, LaNesha Tabb, Tanner Olson, and Alice Lee

Leading with a Humble Heart: A 40-Day Devotional for Leaders by Zac Bauermaster

Recalibrate the Culture: Our Why…Our Work…Our Values by Jimmy Casas

Creating Curious Classrooms: The Beauty of Questions by Emma Chiappetta

Crafting the Culture: 45 Reflections on What Matters Most by Joe Sanfelippo and Jeffrey Zoul

Improving School Mental Health: The Thriving School Community Solution by Charle Peck and Dr. Cameron Caswell

Building Authenticity: A Blueprint for the Leader Inside You by Todd Nesloney And Tyler Cook

Connecting Through Conversation: A Playbook for Talking with Kids by Erika Bare and Tiffany Burns

The Dream Factory: Designing a Purposeful Life by Mark Trumbo

Stories Behind Stances: Creating Empathy Through Hearing The Other Side by Chris Singleton

Happy Eyes: Becoming All Things to All People by Ryan Tillman

The Generative Age: Artificial Intelligence and the Future of Education by Alana Winnick

Recalibrate the Culture: Action Guide by Jimmy Casas

Leading with PEOPLE: A Six Pillar Framework for Fruitful Leadership by Zac Bauermaster

WHOSE PERMISSION ARE YOU WAITING FOR?

A School Leader's Guide to Reclaiming Purpose by Frederick C. Buskey

Foundations of an Elite Culture: Building Success with High Standards and a Positive Environment by David Arencibia

Personalize: Meeting the Needs of All Learners by Eric Sheninger and Nicki Slaugh

The Five Principles of Educator Professionalism: Rebuilding Trust in Schools by Nason Lollar

Words on the Wall: Culturizing Your Classroom For Observable Impact by Jimmy Casas and Cale Birk

School of Engagement: 45 Activities to Ignite Student Learning by Jonathan Alsheimer

Intentional Instructional Moves: Strategic Steps to Accelerate Student Learning by Sherry St. Clair

Overcoming Education: Complex Challenges, Difficult People, and the Art of Making a Difference by Brad R. Gustafson

The Language of Behavior: A Framework to Elevate Student Success by Charle Peck and Joshua Stamper

www.ingramcontent.com/pod-product-compliance
Lightning Source LLC
Chambersburg PA
CBHW070618030426
42337CB00020B/3840